GETTING STARTED

# with
# **seed**
# beads

## Dustin Wedekind

 **INTERWEAVE PRESS**

Interweave Press LLC
201 East Fourth Street
Loveland, CO 80537-5655 USA
www.interweave.com

Printed in China by Asia Pacific Offset.

Photography, Joe Coca.
Text, illustrations, and photography ©2007
  Interweave Press LLC.

Library of Congress Cataloging-in-Publication Data

Wedekind, Dustin, 1971-
  Getting started with seed beads / Dustin Wedekind, author.
    p. cm.
  Includes index.
  ISBN-13: 978-1-59668-016-6 (hardcover)
  1. Beadwork. I. Title.
  TT860.W385 2007
  745.594'2--dc22
                                        2006037053

10 9 8 7 6 5 4 3 2 1

*Thanks to*

Jean Campbell and Stephen Beal, for giving me a beading vocabulary.

Connie Lehman, for planting a seed, followed with decades of nurturing inspiration.

Grandma Lucille, for my first contact with seed beads on a reservation in Montana.

Grandma Eloise, for her custom-tailored sewing skills.

And my dad, for acknowledging the art in everything.

# contents

# introduction

Seed beads are magical. The tiny bits of glass contain worlds in themselves, telling stories and demonstrating ingenuity of people throughout time and around the world. One lone bead might go unnoticed, but gathered together, they make a bold statement. From the simplest little spheres with holes, seed beads can be combined into three-dimensional shapes—solid or airy, practical or decorative, as simple as a few beads on a string or as complicated as a seed-beaded sculpture.

Seen for the first time, seed bead creations might look hopelessly complicated, demanding dexterity, creativity, and patience. But with this book to guide you, you'll soon learn to create elegant and deceptively simple pieces. Do diagrams with crisscrossing paths put you on edge? Think you don't have a creative bone in your body? Relax, it's not rocket science. Starting with all the tools and materials you'll need before progressing to a step-by-step how-to intensive, *Getting Started with Seed Beads* will soon have you weaving seed beads in fantastic arrays.

With the basics under your belt, you can sample over twenty projects that illuminate the most popular of beading techniques. The projects aren't fancy one-hit wonders; they are the building blocks and tools that will get you started on your own path. While it isn't necessary to learn them all, you never know when you'll come across some pattern or color or texture that sparks your creative mind and entices you to try a new technique.

I hope you'll use this book only as the beginning of your own explorations of the world of seed beads. Each tiny bead holds potential, waiting for you to unlock it.

# 1

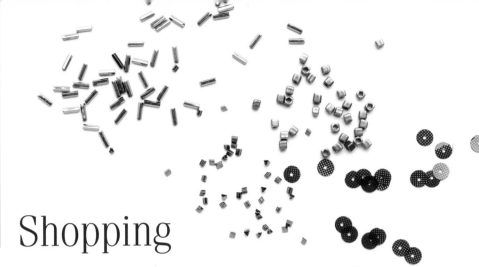

# Shopping

Beads have long been traded for goods and services around the world. Today's technology makes it easier than ever to be a part of this tradition via the Internet, where you can find any bead imaginable from hundreds of vendors. My first hank of seed beads was purchased at a pow-wow from a vendor selling everything from beads to bones to batteries. I didn't know what I would do with the beads, I just liked the way they sparkled and how they felt in my hands. It wasn't long after that I found myself entering a bead store.

## AT FIRST GLANCE

You can probably spot strands of semiprecious stones hanging on a wall, and containers of all kinds of beads are on every possible surface. Made of stone, glass, plastic, bone, horn, and almost anything you can drill a hole through, the beads sold loose in little bins are priced individually. These are a delight to use, but we're here to see the seed beads. They may be sold in tubes, looking like a box of crayons, or tied in hanks, hanging from hooks. While at first they may not look exciting when compared with the multitude of other beads available, seed beads can be every bit as diverse, colorful, and unique.

## BUYING FOR THIS BOOK

Pick up a tray or basket, usually found near the door, which the store has provided for your shopping convenience. You may be surprised how fast your hands are overflowing with choices, and a tray can help you arrange the beads comfortably. Close at hand can usually be found small plastic bags, pens, and tags so that you can write down the prices of your selections. (These are less important for seed beads than loose beads, as the containers or hanks are generally marked with prices.)

# START SHOPPING!

Some beadwork patterns give ingredients in grams or, occasionally, hanks; you will notice that the projects in these pages give more general requirements, like the number of different types of beads to use and what sizes are needed. You will be able to complete any of these projects with a fairly small amount of beads; in fact, there will probably be leftovers in a tube, bag, or hank of beads used for these projects. If you were buying beads for a bigger project, you'd want to make sure to buy all the beads of the same type at the same time because if you were to run out in the middle, you might not find beads to match.

**TIP: Bead Storage** Keep the beads in the packages they come in, storing them within a tackle-type box. Organize by color or shape or size as you deem most useful according to your mode of designing. Don't pour the beads into the tackle box—even though it may have divided sections, dropping the box with loose beads inside could lead to disastrous spillage.

# KNOW YOUR SEED BEADS

The biggest distinction in seed beads is probably Czech vs Japanese. The easiest way to see the difference is in how they're presented: Czech beads are generally sold in hanks, ten to twelve strands of beads bound together with a knot, while Japanese seed beads are sold in grams by the bag, tube, or other container.

## Czech

Czech seed beads, which are generally donut-shaped, have slight irregularities that allow them to fit together organically. Rounded edges and variations in thickness are great for free-form embroidery and circular bead weaving. Hanked beads are handy for projects that use prestrung beads, as they can be transferred directly from the hank onto your bead thread. The thread that the beads are sold on is not suitable for beading. (See page 21 for removing beads from hanks.) This applies to most European beads (from Italy, France, Germany), which tend to be vintage.

In addition to the characteristic donut shape, Czech beads called **charlottes** are wonderful for beadweaving and embroidery. The single facet cut into the side of charlotte beads adds an extra sparkle when light hits the reflective surface.

Czech      Charlotte

There are about 4,000 size 11° beads in a 30-gram hank.

## Japanese

Japanese seed beads are generally more uniform in shape than their European counterparts. Their shape is squarer than Czech beads, nearly twice as wide as a thin Czech bead of the same height. Because of their regular shape, Japanese seed beads are satisfying to work with in stitches where beads fit together very closely, like peyote or brick.

Japan also produces **cylinder beads,** named Delicas, Treasures, or Dynamites according to manufacturer. For even results, you'll love how these beads snap together when working from a graphed-out pattern. They are nearly square when seen from the side and have a large round hole from end to end. The precision means you will rarely have a misshapen bead or one with a hole too small to use, but it will cost you a bit more to build a palette. They're fairly compatible with a size 11° or 12° seed bead.

Japanese    Cylinders

A 6" tube of size 11° beads weighs 30 grams and contains about 3,400 beads, while a 2" tube of size 15° beads weighs about 10 grams and contains 2,600 beads.

A 2" tube of cylinder beads contains about 900 beads.

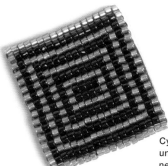

Cylinder beads, shown in the square at left, are very uniform and snap together neatly, while the roundness of Czech beads shows in the right square.

# SIZING UP BEADS

Most Japanese and Czech seed beads are sized following one classification system, a number followed by a degree symbol (referred to in beading as an "aught"). The larger the number, the smaller the bead.

Most common are size 11's, which roughly measure one inch when 11 of them are lined up side by side (not hole to hole). A size 6° is about twice as big, with a size 8° somewhere in between. Going smaller, almost half of an 11°, are size 14°/15's. Though less common, beads ranging from as small as size 24° (stringable only on a hair-thin thread) to as large as a size 2° (workable with a shoelace) are available. Other beads, including cubes and other shapes, are sized using the metric system.

### Mixing sizes

Some designs are worked entirely with a single size of bead, while others benefit from a mix of sizes to create texture and rhythm within a piece of beadwork. If you want smooth beadwork, stick to a single type of bead. Mixing size 11° Czech and Japanese beads will offer you more color choices, but their slight differences in shape may yield a bumpy surface.

Changing the size of beads can change the shape of your piece while maintaining the same number of beads per row. A simple peyote-stitched strip (see page 78) takes shape when worked with size 15's, transitioning to size 11° for a few rows, then size 8's, ending at the top with size 6's and 2's.

The rings shown here demonstrate how gradually increasing the bead size changes the overall shape.

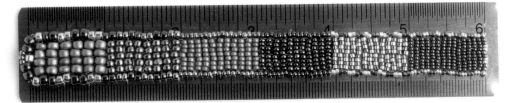

The measure of aughts: Beads are sized by how many of them fit side-by-side within one inch. Shown here are size 6°, size 8°, Japanese size 11°, Czech size 11°, Delica cylinders, and size 15°.

# OTHER SHAPES

**Triangles** and **hexes** are beads whose shapes create texture and a little drama when added to rounded seed beads. Hex beads have six flat sides, sometimes twisted, and make for an industrial feel. Triangles and hexes are easily worked in with seed beads, as they are sized the same way.

**Cubes** can look like mosaic tiles when woven together. Cubes are commonly available in 1.5mm, 3mm, and 4mm sizes.

**Bugle beads**—long tubes of glass—work well in strands and fringe, in openwork such as nets and ladders or sewn onto fabric. They often have sharp edges, so string a round seed bead on each end to protect the thread from being frayed or sliced through.

**Sequins** are produced in abundant colors and shapes for trendy designs. Fun to sew onto cloth, sequins can also be strung along with beads, showing themselves, then hiding, depending on the angle you view them.

**Nailheads** are akin to sequins. Made of pressed glass, each nailhead has a hole running laterally through, or one on each side, for sewing onto cloth. Unfortunately, they are mostly vintage.

**Cabochons,** having no holes, cannot be strung. They have a flat side that is usually glued to another flat surface.

While regular Japanese and Czech seed beads make up most of a seed beader's toolkit, several additional shapes round out the selection, each with its own use.

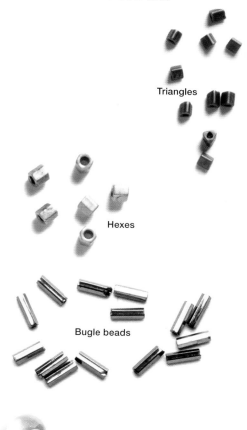

Triangles

Hexes

Bugle beads

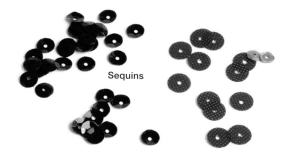

Sequins

Nailheads

Striped seed beads

Beads offer a rainbow of colors, especially when presented in hanks. Most of the colors come from the glass itself, and may be further enhanced with subtle finishes. Some colors are dyed or applied to the surface of the beads and vary in permanence.

# COLORS AND FINISHES

From primary to pastel hues, **opaque** beads offer bold shapes of color, like Pop Art canvases and football uniforms.

**Silver-lined** beads are made with a flashy core that reflects light through colored glass, appearing to be lit from within. With the addition of colorful coatings or matte finishes, they can be as glitzy as the Las Vegas Strip or as subtle as the Milky Way.

For added depth, **color-lined** beads blur the distinction between surface and core, with two colors seemingly occupying the same space.

**Metallic** seed beads are created in several ways, including painting on a metallic coating, electroplating, or galvanizing. Unfortunately, many silver or gold finishes tarnish or wear off, exposing the glass beneath. Ask your bead vendor to be sure.

**Matte finishes** have a soft appearance.

**Iris** and **Aurora Borealis (AB)** finishes coat the bead with a holographic iridescence, like abalone fairies caught in an oil slick.

**Stripes** are formed when glass canes of different colors are pulled together during the beadmaking process. Reminiscent of Old World trading, they mix well with African trade beads.

Metallic seed beads

# NEEDLES

A **beading needle** is a 2-inch-long thin wire with a very small opening at one end to hold a thread. A size 12 is suitable for most beading tasks. Like beads and wire, the larger the number, the smaller the size. For small beads or projects that require many passes of thread through each bead, a size 15 may be required. Use a size 10 when working with heavy thread that won't fit through the eye of a smaller needle or when using beads with larger holes. I find that a heavier needle will help to reduce fatigue that is caused by fussing with a flimsy needle. English John James brand needles are high quality and available in many shapes and sizes. I like size 11 Indian-made Pony brand needles because they accommodate most threads and fit through most beads several times.

**Sharps** and **Glovers** are also common beading needles. Sharps are shorter, about 1" (2.5 cm) long, and may be preferred by small hands. Glovers come from glove makers, having ridges that help the needle pass through leather.

When fitting bulky fibers or ribbons through beads, use a **twisted-wire needle.** These are sold as a fine wire whose ends have been twisted together, creating an open loop of an eye. The needle is a bit flimsy, and you can easily make one yourself if needed in a pinch (even with a paper clip!).

Unless specifically noted, all the projects in this book use black size B or D Nymo thread and a size 10 or 12 beading needle, depending on the size of beads that are used.

# THREAD

**Nymo** is a synthetic (nylon) thread borrowed from the upholstery world, having proved its strength through use by the industry. Bead stores carry the thread as bobbins in many colors and sizes, with D being largest, B a medium, and 0 or 00 as fine thread. C-lon is a comparable name brand offering many delicious hues; it glides smoothly but tends to fray a bit more than the Nymo thread.

**Silamide** is made of multiple nylon threads and is generally a thicker, twistier version of the same.

**Braided beading thread** is gaining popularity with beaders. Most of these threads (including PowerPro and Dandyline) originated as fishing lines. These super-strong lines are supple yet behave more like sewing thread. These threads are great for any project that doesn't require much weaving through beads, though some beaders will swear by their 6-lb test for all their needle-weaving techniques. Use sharp scissors and hold the thread taut when cutting it to avoid a frayed end.

### Waxes and conditioners

**Thread conditioner** will help to avoid tangles. Thread Heaven is a silicone-based product that causes the thread to repel itself, making tangles scarce while helping to slide the thread through a bead's hole. A traditional thread conditioner, **beeswax** tends to stick the thread to itself, but has the quality of adding a feeling of strength to the beadwork. **Synthetic beeswax (microcrystalline wax)** is available and advisable to use, as it will add to the longevity of your work without attracting bugs.

Strong enough for a woman, but made for a man, these braided fishing lines should stand up to all your rugged beading needs.

# FINDINGS

"Findings" are all the little pieces, usually made of metal, that are used to finish jewelry.

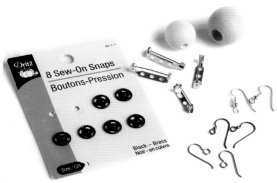

**Ear wires** can be attached with a loop of seed beads to make the smallest sample of beadwork into jewelry.

**Pin backs** are useful for making quick last-minute gifts. Embroidered buttons, wire flowers, and even beads glued onto paper can be attached to a pin back to create a brooch.

**Buttons** can accent a garment or secure the closure on a piece of jewelry. Glass, metal, plastic, fancy, plain, painted, carved, molded, drilled, or shanked, you can find a button as expressive as your beadwork. Or, you might be inspired by the button and find beads to string around it.

**Sew-on snaps**, usually black or silver-colored nickel or clear nylon plastic, come in different sizes and make great closures.

**Craft wire** in assorted colors, 24- or 26-gauge, is used for making flowers in this book. Wire provides a self-supporting thread for beads, allowing you to use it in many places.

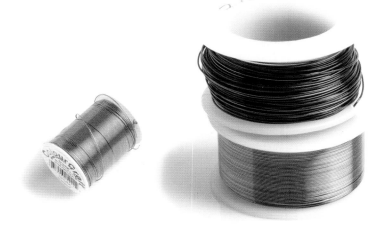

Some of the items helpful for happy beading will be available at your local craft store.

# BEADING FOUNDATIONS

Some surfaces are more accepting of beads than others. Whatever you are beading onto, be sure that it is not prone to environmental degradation, rotting away from under the beads. Densely woven fabrics support bead embroidery; loosely woven fabrics may buckle under the tension of beading thread, forming gaps between the woven threads. Nonwoven grounds, like felt or interfacing, are great ways to avoid that problem. Use them also to back a thin fabric to stabilize it for beading. Eazy Felt and Lacy's Stiff Stuff are stiff and easy to bead. Wooden beads, Styrofoam, and tins are other beadable surfaces used in this book.

### Adhesive and glue

**Double-sided craft tape,** like Terrifically Tacky Tape, cures to permanence like glue and is acid free, making it great for beading. It's available in rolls of various widths as well as flat sheets that can be cut to fit. Avoid using beads that have an applied finish—the finish will stick to the tape but the beads will not. Avoid touching the tape by applying it in small sections or keep the protective paper covering and use a knife to expose sections as you work.

**Jeweler's cement** (G-S Hypo or E-6000) are industrial adhesives that hold beads and cabochons to your work.

**Eazy Felt and Lacy's Stiff Stuff are stiff and easy to bead.**

# TOOLS

**Sharp scissors** are essential. Dull blades don't give a smooth trim, so you might never get thread through a needle. Neat trimming is also needed when finishing, clipping short tails close to the beadwork.

**Needle-nose pliers** will help pull a needle through a tight bead. If the bead is very tight, back the needle out and find a different path around that bead (or use a smaller needle); if you force the needle through, you could bust the bead and damage the thread that was inside it.

**Wire cutters** and **round-nose pliers** are handy if you are working with wire. Round-nose pliers help to make smooth, even loops and bends.

**Graph paper, markers, and pencils** are all useful to have on hand, to make notes on the project you're working on (or record your inspiration for a new one!).

**Embroidery scissors**

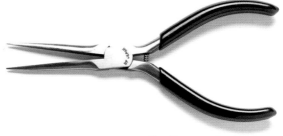

**Round-nose pliers**

**Needle-nose pliers**

A tray with a Vellux liner makes a useful beading surface.

# Getting Started

Once you've made your selections at the bead shop, you'll want to go home and play with your new treasures.

Between purchasing the perfect beads and assembling them into your dream project, there are a few steps to ensure that your beading time will be enjoyable.

Whether you work at your kitchen table or from the couch, be sure to sit comfortably and give yourself plenty of light. You'll need an even, steady surface to spread out your beads. Portable lighting and portable lap trays are investments that can help you with other tasks beyond beading.

## On the mat

Don't forget something to put the beads in or on. A beading mat can be a kitchen towel or scrap of felt, something that will prevent the beads from rolling or bouncing around. A Vellux blanket is spongy and has a pile (like carpet) rather than loops of thread (like a towel), which prevents your needle from getting snagged. If you may need to move your beadwork while in the middle of a project, cut the mat to fit inside a shallow tray.

## Triangle scoop

If you are beading on a mat, keep a triangle scoop handy for shifting beads around. To move small piles of beads, drag the triangle's edge across the mat, press the edge into the mat to scoop them up, and point the triangle into a bag to pour them in.

## Bead bowls

To keep beads from rolling all over, you may find it useful to pour them into bowls, dipping into them like an array of Easter-egg dyes. My favorite beading bowl is made of wood, probably intended for holding salad. It is shallow, so I don't have to reach down into it to get beads, and the beads have room to spread out, making it easy to find the right color. The texture of the wood keeps the beads from sliding around and absorbs vibrations so that the beads don't bounce about and over the edges. (Plastic bowls are bouncy and slippery.) I also love vintage crystal coasters with silver rims or souvenir ashtrays: The heavy glass won't easily tip over, the beads have room to spread apart, and you can stack many coasters without crushing the beads inside.

My favorite wooden beading bowl

## De-hanking

Hanks of beads are delightful—not just to look at, but they give you a better idea of how the beads are going to look when worked than if you were looking through a tube or bag. The disadvantage is that you can't pull just a few beads from a hank; you have to cut a thread and release a whole strand. Get a bowl to hold the hank. Select one of the strands and cut it free, letting it fall into the bowl; if you try holding on to it, you will be left holding a few beads while the thread falls through, flinging beads around like a wet noodle. So, with the strand in the bowl, slowly pull the thread free. Slowly.

A crystal coaster

## Re-bagging

Make a funnel by rolling a piece of paper into a cone shape. Hold it with a bag or tube at the bottom in one hand and pick up the bowl with your other hand to pour the beads into the bag.

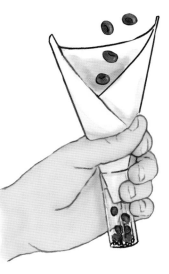

Now that you're all set up, you can begin the fun part: the beading. Some rules of beading apply to craftsmanship, while most others are really just matters of preference.

# START BEADING

## The thread

Pull an arm's length of thread (3 to 4 feet) from the bobbin, then condition it by running wax or Thread Heaven across it. Stretch the thread by pulling it between thumb and finger several times to de-curl it. Cut the thread at an angle with sharp scissors to help it go through the eye of the needle.

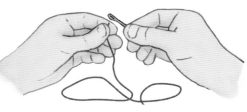

It might seem that you could avoid the challenge of threading a beading needle multiple times in the same piece (and the tedium of weaving in thread tails when you finish) by using a really long thread, more than 6' (2 m). However, a long thread gets tangled more often and gets worn by weaving through more beads, making it frayed and fragile by the time you are near the end of the thread.

## The needle

"Needle to thread" is the best way to describe threading a beading needle: Pinch the thread near the end, then lower the needle down to it.

### TIP: Needle Troubleshooting

• You may find that sucking the end of the thread to a point will help, or even biting the thread with your teeth to mash it flat, to get it through the eye of the needle.

• Rotate the needle—eyes are punched through the metal from one side to make the hole, causing one side of the needle to have a larger hole.

• With use, the eye of a needle will collapse, so switch it out with a new needle fresh from the package.

• Still can't get it threaded? Try a larger needle!

*Getting Started with Seed Beads*

## Stringing

Pour beads out onto a mat or into a shallow bowl. Hold the needle between your thumb and middle finger; stab the point of the needle into the hole of the bead and use your index finger to flick the bead up the needle. Continue adding beads to the needle, holding them in place with your thumb until 6–8 beads are on, then slide them down the thread.

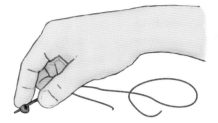

## The tension bead

A tension bead (also called a stopper bead) keeps your beads from sliding off the end of the thread without the use of knots; it is usually removed after you have some beadwork started. To create a tension bead, string 1 seed bead onto the needle, then hold the bead with your other hand and slide it down toward the end of the thread, usually about 4" (10 cm) from the end. Hold both ends of the thread so that it is tight against the inside of the bead to avoid piercing the thread with the needle, then pass the needle through the bead again (in the same direction) and pull snug.

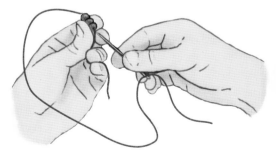

## Tails

The end of the thread that is closest to the needle is your "working thread." At the other end, a "tail thread" marks the start of your work and serves as something to hold onto when getting the beadwork going. You may also have a tail thread when adding new thread to continue working. Either way, they need to be long enough that they may be woven back into the work when finished, about 4–6" (10–12 cm). Hold the beads in place near the end of the thread with one hand while you pass the needle through with your other hand, the same as threading a tension bead.

## PASS THROUGH AND PASS BACK THROUGH

When you string a bead, you are passing through from one side of the bead to the other. If you turn the needle around and pass back through the bead, it will come off the thread. "Pass through" and "pass back through" are used to signify which direction the thread passes through beads. Imagine painting an arrow on each bead as you string it, indicating which way it was strung. The arrow won't change, even if you pass back through the bead. The figures in this book are drawn with the bead holes facing the needle, showing which direction they were strung.

String 4 beads and pass through the first one again to form a loop; pass *back* through the first one to form a picot.

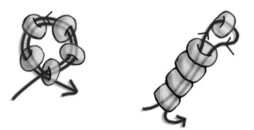

To make a circle of beads, pass through all of them again; to make a fringe, pass *back* through the beads (except the last bead added, to prevent the thread from passing back out of all the beads).

# ADDING THREAD

Keep an eye on your thread and pause when you have about 6" (15 cm) of working thread remaining. You can usually start and stop threads at any time, anywhere in the beadwork; if you are working a tubular stitch, you may want to try finishing the current round so that you don't have to remember where you are in the pattern. For flat work, stop in the middle of the row, which keeps the edges neat and is more secure because the ends of the thread are surrounded by worked beads.

When you're ready to end a thread, weave through beads in the previous rows, working back and forth across the piece and retracing your thread path. Pull the needle off the thread, leaving the tail to show where the end is. Put the needle on a new thread and pass through beads near the old tail. Pull most of the thread through beads, leaving a new short tail (2" [5 cm] if you won't be knotting, 6" [15 cm] if knotting is required). Cover that tail with your thumb to hold it in place as you weave through beads following the path of the old thread until you exit from the last worked bead, then continue beading where you left off. When finished, trim the old and new tails close to the work if they are secure, or use a needle to weave them through and tie knots if necessary before trimming.

There is a rhythm to beading, stringing beads and passing through beads, counting both actions, and so on. Then there is the rhythm of the thread, which inevitably will need to be replenished for beading projects larger than a shot glass.

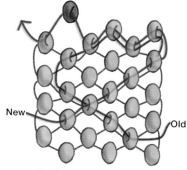

Weave the old thread back through the work.

Begin a new thread, anchoring the tail in the work.

## KNOTTING

If you are working with large beads, or if the work is fairly loose or open, you may need to secure the thread with a few knots. To do so, weave back through a few beads and pull the thread snug. Pass the tip of the needle under the worked thread between the beads that you are exiting from. Pull the needle through under that thread, and pass through the loop that is formed by the working thread—you have formed a half hitch knot. Pull snug, and pass through the next few beads. Tie another half hitch knot, pass through a few more beads, tie a third knot, pass through a few more beads, then pull the thread tight and trim close to the work.

## SNARLS AND TANGLES

If the thread tangles, it has probably formed a slipknot that can be pulled free. If it is truly a tangled mess, hold it gently between your fingers and tease it apart by wiggling the needle in the mess. The thread tends to get twisted as you work, so most tangles can be avoided by letting the work hang free and pulling the thread through your fingers to untwist it.

## FINISHING

You've been beading for hours when, all of a sudden, you're done! Congratulations. But you're not finished yet. Take care when finishing to ensure a long-lasting piece that doesn't go to pieces. Start by reinforcing the last row or round by passing through the beads again, being sure to follow the same thread path. Not following the thread path could pull the beads out of line and distort the work. Continue weaving through beads, switching direction now and then so that the thread puts tension on itself, making it difficult to pull out. If the beadwork is dense, weaving in the ends should be sufficient to hold.

**TIP:** However you reach your final beading project, one thing to keep in mind is "no exposed thread." If the thread shows, it is exposed to the elements and could be harmed, causing all your work to fall apart. Bead doom.

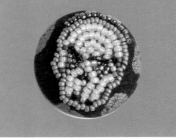

*Getting Started with Seed Beads*

# ADDING CLOSURES

## Button

String a short column of beads to form a shank so that the loop will fit underneath it. String the button, then pass back through the column of beads and into the beadwork. Weave through the beadwork and the column and button several times to reinforce. For 2-holed buttons, string a few beads on top of the button between the holes to protect the thread **(Figure 1)**. With 4 holes, string beads between 2 of the holes, weave through the column of beads, then pass back up to exit the third hole. String 1 bead and pass through the middle of the first set of beads; string another bead and pass through the fourth hole **(Figure 2)**.

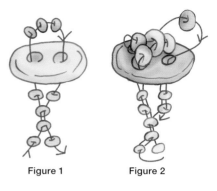

Figure 1      Figure 2

## Loop

At the other end of the beadwork, string enough beads to fit snug around the button. Test the size of the loop before securing it, then pass through it several times to reinforce **(Figure 3)**. Add some design flair while reinforcing the loop: string 1 bead, pass through 1 bead, string 1 bead, pass through 1 bead, etc. **(Figure 4)**. Or, for a square-stitched loop, string 1 bead and pass back through 1 bead and through the bead just strung **(Figure 5)**. Repeat all around, then pass through all the added beads to reinforce the loop.

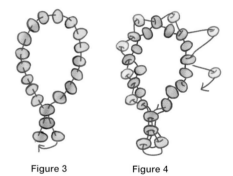

Figure 3      Figure 4

Figure 5

# Daisy Chain Demo

Let's use the humble daisy chain to go over beading terminology in a step-by-step intensive. After giving each direction as you'll find it in the rest of the book (and in most other beading patterns), we will walk through every step, so that next time you face a pattern you can decipher those confusing directions for yourself.

## Materials

Size 8° beads in each of three colors (A, B, C)

Thread

Needle

2 eyeglasses leash findings

This section tells you what you will use in the course of the project. With beading thread and some wire, it is assumed that you have an ample supply on hand to finish the project. For this book, you won't find a specific quantity of seed beads listed; just have a hank or tube on hand of each kind of bead specified. This section also lists the pliers, needles, and anything else you'll need to have on hand to complete the project. Since this is a simple project, a needle is the only tool needed.

**To begin:** Choose three bead colors, assign each one a letter (A, B, or C), and pour some of each onto your mat or into a bowl. Choose a thread to match the bead colors and cut a piece that is long as is comfortable for you to work with (about 4–6' [1–2 m] or no longer than your arm can reach once the needle is threaded). Stretch the thread by pulling it tightly through your fingers several times. Thread a beading needle and pull about one-third of the thread through it. If this is to be a heavier project, you may condition your thread with beeswax, or use Thread Heaven to smooth the thread for a lighter project.

**1. String 8A and pass through them again, leaving a 6" tail** (Figure 1).
Use the needle to string 8 beads in the color you chose for A, then hold on to them with your other hand and slide them toward the end of the thread. Continue holding the beads while you pass the needle through them again in the same direction, beginning with the first bead strung. Hold the beads and the tail thread as you pull the needle through and snug the beads into a circle. You don't have to pass through all of them at once; you may pass through the first few and pull the thread snug, then pass through the remaining beads. Keep hold of the tail thread while you work, which keeps it (and your beadwork) out of the way and prevents tangling with the working thread. You will have more tangles if you keep the work flat on the table.

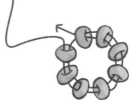

Figure 1

**2. *String 1C and pass back through the opposite 2 beads** (Figure 2).
The previous thread path is now shown in blue; follow the path indicated by the red thread to string 1C and pass the needle in the opposite direction, back through 2 beads opposite where the thread is exiting from, and pull snug. You don't have to slide a bead down to the work as soon as you've strung it, just keep your eye on the beads that you are passing through and the strung beads will fall into place as you snug the thread. The asterisk marks the point where you begin a repeated sequence and will be referred to in a later step.

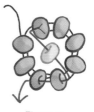

Figure 2

**3. String 2B and pass back through the last 2 beads and through the 2 beads just strung** (Figure 3). String 2B and pass back through the same 2 beads just passed through (which is the same direction just traveled, but is the opposite direction of the bead's initial stringing direction); pull the thread snug so that the 2 beads just strung are in position for you to pass through them again.

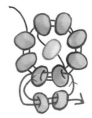

Figure 3

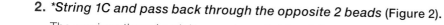

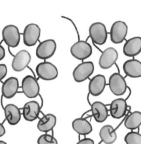

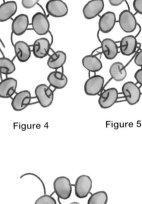

Figure 4          Figure 5

Figure 6

4. *String 6B and pass through the last 2 beads and the 6 beads just strung* (**Figure 4**). String 6B beads and pass through the last 2 beads that you passed through, pull snug, and continue through all 6 beads in the same direction to complete and reinforce another circle of beads.

5. *Pass through the next 2 beads. String 1C and pass back through the opposite 2 beads* (**Figure 5**). Pass through the 2 beads immediately in front of the bead that the thread is exiting from, going in the same direction as the thread is headed, and pull snug. String 1C and pass back through the 2 beads that are opposite the last 2 beads passed through.

6. *String 2A and pass back through the last 2 beads and through the 2 beads just strung. String 6A and pass through the last 2 beads and the 6 beads just strung. Pass through all the beads in the same direction to complete another circle of beads* (**Figure 6**). This combines Steps 2 and 3 to make the same stitch as the second daisy, using a different color bead.

7. *Repeat from * for the desired length.* The asterisk indicates the start of a repeated sequence. Return to that point (here, the beginning of Step 2) and repeat the steps again until the work is as long as you need it to be before moving on to the next step. (In some patterns, you will be instructed to repeat from the asterisk a given number of times.)

*Getting Started with Seed Beads*

**8.** *Pass the end of the chain through one half of the clasp; fold the end over and weave through beads to secure* (Figure 7). *Repeat with the tail thread, and trim.* In this case, one half of the clasp is one of the eyeglasses leashes. Pass the end of the daisy chain and the working thread through a leash, far enough that you can fold the end over. Use the working thread to weave through beads where the end meets the chain, and the end itself, several times to secure. Remember to follow existing thread paths as much as possible to avoid distorting the beadwork or allowing exposed thread. If the needle won't fit through beads, try a smaller needle and pass through as best you can. Weave back through beads and pull snug while you trim the thread close to the work. Put a needle on the tail thread and repeat to attach the other half of the clasp.

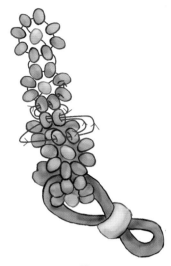

Figure 7

## When to add thread

What isn't covered in the step-by-step instruction is how or when to add thread. Variations in bead size, thread tension, and personal preferences all make adding thread hard to predict. Stop stitching when your working thread is 4–6" long. Don't wait until it is too short to work with— you need enough thread to work back through a few stitches, which is hard to do if the thread is shorter than the needle. To end the thread in daisy chain, weave the needle through beads of the last daisy and tie an overhand knot around the thread that connects two beads. Weave through the next daisy and tie another knot, then weave through a few more beads **(Figure 8)**. Put the needle on a new length of thread and weave through the last few daisies, tying knots between beads. Continue working with the new thread, then cut the tail threads when finished **(Figure 9)**.

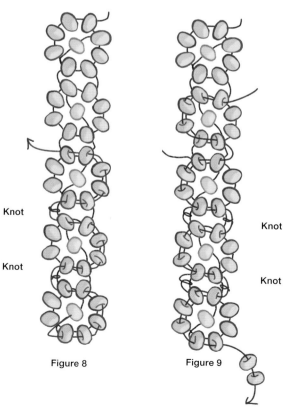

Knot

Knot

Knot

Knot

Figure 8          Figure 9

# Glue

"Are those all glued on?" No. "They're stitched?" No, not really! Beadwork can be mystifying to the uninitiated—densely beaded embroideries look glued together, while beads attached with glue may look like they've been stitched to an impenetrable metal gas can.

If you have ever tried to glue a bead to something, you may have noticed that the bead will want to go anywhere *but* on the glue. And once the glue is dry, a bead's smooth surface prevents the glue from forming a truly secure bond. These projects use sewing aids—pins and thread—to keep the beads organized and in place while the adhesive is given time to bond, and they remain in place to hold the beads together. Another extremely useful aid is double-sided craft tape, which is super sticky and cures like glue in 24 hours. Whether using glue or tape, work in small sections, adding more adhesive as you go, keeping your tack tacky and your fingers clean.

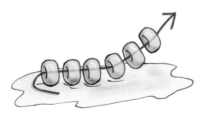

# Bead Soup Cans

## Materials

Seed beads in assorted sizes and finishes

Flat-backed bead, nailhead, or cabochon

Round tin, shown here 2" (5 cm) in diameter

Needle and thread

Double-sided craft tape

You may not be able to bead just one of these cute tins so make one for each of your favorite colors. Store the tins on magnetic strips attached to the wall and pull one down when you need just a pinch of yellow, or green, or browns to accent a project. You can easily mix bead sizes with this technique, creating tons of texture.

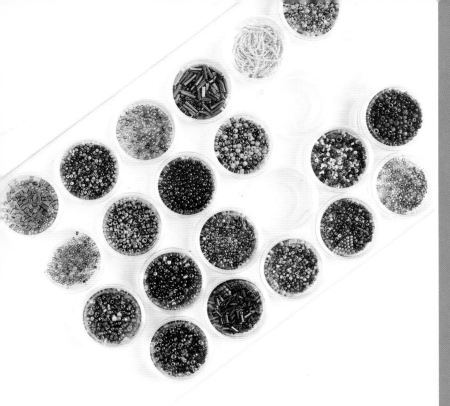

## Bead Soup

When you've finished with a beaded project, you might have a small pile of assorted beads in complementary shapes, sizes, colors, and finishes. Instead of sorting them back into their individual tubes or bags, keep them combined together as "bead soup." The combination might inspire you to dream up another project, or you may decide to make another piece to match, like earrings to complement a necklace. You can premix your beads to get an even mix of colors or textures, then string beads at random from this mix of "soup."

*Getting Started with Seed Beads*

## Lid sides.

**1.** Cover the top and sides of the lid with an even single layer of tape; keep the top covered with the protective backing while you work the sides.

**2.** Use 6' (2 m) of thread to string 1 bead and pass through it again to form a tension bead, leaving a 2" (5 cm) tail. String about 1" (2.5 cm) of beads and slide them down to the tension bead. Hold the tail and working threads to keep the beads snug while you press the beads to the tape along the bottom lip of the lid **(Figure 1)**. Use the tip of the needle to press the tail thread to the tape so that it is secure. (The tail will be covered with beads when you are finished.)

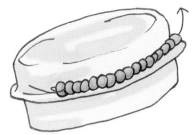

Figure 1

**3.** String more beads and lift the needle up so that the beads slide down the thread while you rotate the tin with your other hand, letting the beads fall into place. Repeat around the lid until you reach the start of the round, then pass through a few of the first beads strung and pull snug. It is better to have too few beads in a round: If you try to squeeze another bead in to fill the space, it will most likely pop up and ruin a smooth finish, possibly causing more beads to come off with it.

Figure 2

**4.** Working in the opposite direction of the previous round, string beads and lay them down for another round **(Figure 2)**. Repeat for a third round, which should bring you to the top edge of the lid.

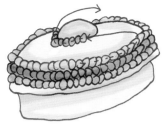

Figure 3

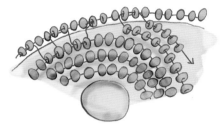

Figure 4

## Lid top

**5.** Expose the tape and place the cabochon or marble in the center of the lid. Bring the working thread across the lid and lay it next to the cabochon. (It is easier to bead around an object than it is to fill inward.) String beads and lay them down next to the cabochon, spiraling out toward the edge **(Figure 3)**. For *circles*, string one round of beads and pass through the first few to hold the circle together, then string another round and repeat. To make a *spiral*, simply wrap the beads round and round. If you hit one point on the edge before the other sides—for example, if your cabochon is off-center—pass through one of the nearest side beads, then work back in the opposite direction toward the other edge **(Figure 4)**. Repeat back and forth or round and round to cover the top of the lid.

## Lid edge

**6.** Press firmly on all the beads to be sure they are stuck down. If you find any loose beads (due to gaps in the tape), work the needle and thread toward these beads and pass through them and the surrounding beads as necessary to keep them from wiggling. Weave through the beads all around the edge, both top beads and side beads, so that the edge beads are firmly held in place. When you are satisfied the beads aren't going anywhere, simply trim your thread close to the work.

**Tip:** If you are covering an object that will be handled frequently or subjected to some other abuse (like a beaded mailbox), protect the finished beadwork with a few coats of Mod Podge or other acrylic sealer.

# Curiously Beaded Tin

## Materials

Size 8°, 11°, and 15° seed beads
Double-sided craft tape
Beading needle and thread

Recycle those mint tins into portable studios—many are just the right size to hold beads, thread, and scissors for beading on the go. Add a magnet to the inside of the lid to keep needles neat. (The technique is the same as for the Soup Cans, with some alterations to accommodate the rectangular lid.)

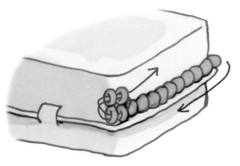

**Figure 1**

### Lid sides

**1.** Cover the top and sides of the lid with an even single layer of tape; to allow the box to open fully, do not cover the back side of the lid. Keep the protective paper on the top of the lid while you work the sides.

**2.** String a bead and pass through it again to form a tension bead, leaving a 2" (5 cm) tail. String about 1" (2.5 cm) of size 11° beads and stick them at the start of the tape, resting them against the lip of the lid. String, then stick beads all around for the first row.

**3.** To secure the start of a new row, string 2 beads and pass through the last 2 beads of the previous row; pull snug and pass through the 2 just strung **(Figure 1)**. Continue to string beads, placing them above the previous row, to the end of the tape. Secure the end of the row by passing through the first 2 beads of the previous row, then through the last 2 beads of this row.

**4.** Repeat Step 3 to work a third row. End the third row by passing through a few beads of the second row, then through the third row to exit near a back corner of the lid.

*Getting Started with Seed Beads*

## Corduroy lid

**5.** Remove the covering to expose the tape on the top of the lid. String enough size 11's to reach from the back corner to the front of the lid near the center; pass through 1 or 2 beads of the top row of side beads to secure the thread **(Figure 2a)**.

**6.** String size 15's and place them alongside those just worked back toward the corner **(Figure 2b)**; pass through side beads to secure the thread. Continue back and forth to fill one corner of the lid, working one row 11's, one row 8's, one row 11's, one row 15's, to create a corduroy texture **(Figure 3)**.

**7.** Pass through beads along the side to exit next to the first row worked on the top. Fill the rest of the lid, securing each row along the back edge the same way as you did for the side rows **(Figure 2c)**. When the lid is completely covered, weave through several beads to secure the thread, and trim close.

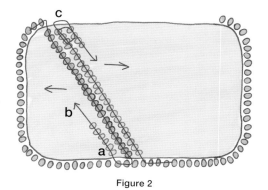

Figure 2

8°  11°  15°  11°  8°  11°  15°  11°  8°

Figure 3

Using these techniques, try out different designs and tins.

# Spangled Eggs

Styrofoam is easy to work with, is available in many shapes, and can easily be carved into new forms. Sequins (spangles) are held in place with short straight pins stuck into the foam. A bit of glue on the business end of the pin holds all secure.

## Materials

Size 11°–6° seed beads
Assorted 4–6mm sequins
Styrofoam egg, 2⁷⁄₁₆" (6 cm) × 1¹³⁄₁₆" (4.6 cm)
About 200 straight ¾" (2 cm) pins

White craft glue
Scrap of cardboard
Marker
Tape measure

1. Wrap the tape measure around the egg and mark the circumference with equal distances (six 1" [2.5 cm] sections for these eggs) on alternating sides of the tape measure. Connect each point with a V to make a zigzag line **(Figure 1)**.

Figure 1

2. Squirt a small puddle of glue onto the cardboard.

3. Use a pin to string 1 bead and 1 sequin. Hold the sequin at the head of the pin while you drag the tip of the pin through the glue **(Figure 2)**. Stick the pin into the egg at one of the zigzag points. Load up another pin and stick it through on the line, next to the edge of the previous sequin so that it overlaps **(Figure 3)**. Continue following the line once around the egg using sequins of the same color **(Figure 4)**.

Figure 2

4. Work the next round using a different color; place each sequin so that it overlaps both the previous sequin and a bit of the previous round to avoid gaps.

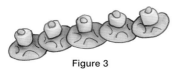

Figure 3

5. Repeat Step 4 along the other side of the first round. Continue working rounds on either side of the first round toward each end of the egg until it is completely covered.

6. Hide your spangled egg someplace quiet (letting the glue dry overnight) until it is found by some lucky bunny. For a hanging egg, load a pin with sequin and glue and stick it through the ends of a folded ribbon and into the top of the egg.

Figure 4

# 4 Embroidery

Bead embroidery can be one of the most straightforward and forgiving applications for seed beads. If you can stitch it, you can probably stitch beads to it!

Add beads to almost any fabric with backstitch or simple running stitch, or attaching spangles or fringe. Some general tips for adding beads to fabric:

⤺ Wash your fabric before beading, to clean it and also to preshrink the fibers. Beaded fabric can usually be handwashed.

⤺ Check for bead colorfastness. Soak them in a bit of water and set them out on a white paper towel. If you see any color on the towel, the beads could also discolor your fabric.

⤺ Use interfacing on the back of thin fabrics to provide a more secure base for the beads.

⤺ Use fabric pens, pencils, chalks, and an assortment of transfer papers that are available to help you get your design outlined on the fabric.

⤺ Use a strong thread and knot often because the piece might encounter a lot of abuse in regular use.

⤺ Plan the location of the beads carefully—a friend probably wouldn't want to receive a handkerchief with a bead-embroidered monogram.

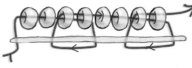
Backstitch

Simple running stitch

Stacks, spangles, or fringe

# Coffee Press Cozy

## Materials

Size 11° seed beads

3 pieces of fabric, each
   measuring 9×14" (23×36 cm)
   (see fabric suggestions at right)

Straight pins

2 pieces of ribbon or
   fabric strip, each
   8" (20 cm)

Fabric marking pencil

Ruler

Sewing needle and thread

Beading needle and thread to
   match front fabric

Iron

Sewing machine (optional)

This useful project includes a few materials beyond beads and thread. The fabric panel is made of three layers, which could easily be recycled from your closet: a solid top layer to contrast with the beads, a flannel middle layer to keep coffee or tea warm, and a cotton print for the back layer to camouflage your stitches. The layers are quilted together with a 3-bead running stitch that can take you in many directions.

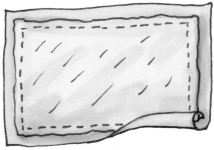

Figure 1

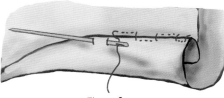

Figure 2

## Quilt panel

**1.** Wash and press the fabrics. Stack them with the right side of the cotton print and the solid color facing out and the flannel sandwiched in the middle. Use straight pins to hold the layers while you use the sewing needle and thread to baste them together.

**2.** With the solid fabric face up, use a fabric pencil to mark a 6½ × 12" (17 × 30 cm) rectangle in the center. Use a sewing machine, or small handstitches, to stitch along this line. Trim the solid and flannel fabrics to ¼" (6 mm) all around. Fold the backing fabric edges over the cut edges, then fold again to cover the stitched line **(Figure 1)**. Use the iron to press the folds and use pins to hold them in place.

**3.** Use the sewing needle and thread to slip-stitch around all four folded edges, passing between the layers of fabric to hide the thread **(Figure 2)**. Leave the basting stitches in place to hold the layers of fabric together while you bead.

## Beaded running stitch

**4.** Use the fabric pencil to mark three or four points evenly within the rectangle that will become the centers of each beaded circle.

**5.** With 6' (2 m) of beading thread and the beading needle work a tailor's knot **(Figure 3)** to secure the thread on the back (patterned) side near one of the pencil marks. (Directions for making a tailor's knot are given at left.)

**6.** Pass through to the front at the mark and string 1 size 8° and 1 size 11°; pass back through the size 8° and to the back **(Figure 4)**. Pull snug and pass through to the front, about ⅜" (1 cm) away from the last stitch.

**7.** Draw a circle ⅝" (1.5 cm) in diameter around the size 8°, starting with where the thread is exiting. String 3 size 11°s and slide them down the thread to the fabric. Pass through to the back along the chalk line, just past the last bead. Pull snug, then pass through to the front about ⅛" (3 mm) in front of the last stitch along the line **(Figure 5)**. Repeat to work along the circle with dashed 3-bead stitches.

**8.** Pass through to the front about ⅜" (1 cm) outside the previous circle. Draw a larger circle around the first circle, then stitch along the line following the directions in Step 7 **(Figure 6)**. Once this circle has been completely stitched around, tie a tailor's knot at the back before beginning the next circle. This will help save beads from being lost if the thread breaks during use. Repeat this step to work 5–6 concentric circles, then begin another grouping at one of the other points.

**10.** When the beaded circles begin to intersect each other, work curved rows of stitches back and forth to fill in between the circles **(Figure 7)**. End the thread by tying several tailor's knots.

**11.** Sew an 8" (20 cm) ribbon or fabric strip to each top two corners along one long side, then tie them together to hold the cozy wrapped around the coffee press.

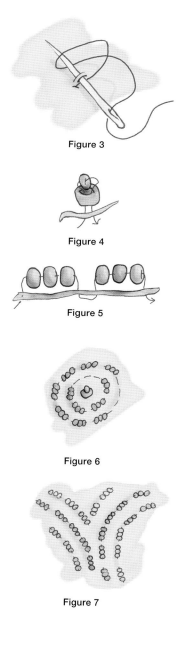

Figure 3

Figure 4

Figure 5

Figure 6

Figure 7

# Bead-a-bet Buttons

Put your mark on what's yours and let them see you coming with an added bit of flair. A few rows of simple backstitch beading can liven up your livery and dress up your denim. Craft and fabric stores sell kits with metal button faces to cover with beaded fabric, then pop its metal shank onto the back to secure the fabric.

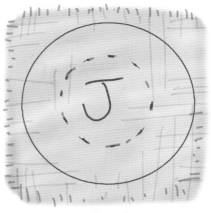

**Figure 1**

### Prepare the backing

1. Cut a piece of freezer paper the same size as the fabric. Place the wrong side of the fabric on the shiny side of the paper and use the iron to fuse them together. (The wax on the paper will stabilize the fabric while you work, then will be torn away after beading.)

2. Place the button face in the center of the fabric and trace around it. Draw another circle around it, twice as wide as the button. Draw a simple single-lined letter inside the circle **(Figure 1)**. With the needle and thread, pass through the paper and fabric from back to front along the drawn line, then pass back through and tie a knot with the tail thread.

## Backstitch

**3.** Pass through to the front at the start of a line of your letter. String 4A, slide them down to the fabric and hold the thread taut along the drawn line; use the tip of the needle to nudge the beads into position and pass through the fabric on the drawn line, slightly in front of the last bead **(Figure 2)**. Pull snug, holding the thread at the back while you pass through to the front between the second and third beads, being sure to come up along the drawn line. Pull snug and pass through the last 2 beads. Repeat, stringing 4A for each stitch and passing through the last 2 to keep the beads in a straight line **(Figure 3)**. At the end of the drawn line, string only enough beads as necessary to finish the line, then pass to the back and then to the front at the start of the next line. Backstitch each line of the letter using A beads.

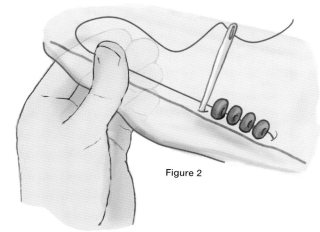

Figure 2

Figure 3

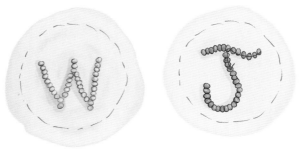

Figure 4

**4.** Pass through the beads on the surface of the fabric to help them stay lined up evenly. Where lines intersect, pass through beads of one line, then directly into the other line to snug the lines together **(Figure 4)**. Pass through all the beads at least once, stitching through the fabric as necessary.

**5.** Add dimension to the letter by stitching a contrasting color along one side of each beaded line. When stitching the second line, pass up through the fabric between the lines of beads, so that the thread pulls the new beads snug **(Figure 5)**. After stitching, pass through the beads again to align them, stitching through beads of both lines, especially at the ends, to snug the lines together **(Figure 6)**.

Figure 5

### Finish the buttons

**6.** Secure the thread by tying several half hitch knots on the back of the fabric and trim leaving a 1" (2.5 cm) tail. Cut the fabric along the outer circle, then tear the freezer paper away around the stitches. (Paper can remain under the stitches, but it shouldn't extend past the edge of the button line.) Holding the button face centered behind the stitches, press the button into the back/shank piece according to manufacturer's instructions.

Figure 6

*Getting Started with Seed Beads*

# Playing with Paisley

## Materials

Assorted sizes (8°, 11°, 15°)
and colors of seed beads
and sequins

Paisley silk necktie
Beading needle and thread to
match the darkest color in
the fabric

Menswear may not ordinarily be dazzled with beads, but look no further than a necktie for a perfect canvas to embellish. While any patterned fabric can serve as the base for bead embroidery, abandoned neckwear offers a ready resource of silk, a strong and brilliant fiber. Readymade ties are lined to help hold their shape, allowing you to bead directly on their surfaces.

## Plan your design

**1.** Take a moment to study the pattern of the fabric—look at the colors, the width of lines, and shapes that combine to make larger shapes. Pick out three main colors and try to match them in bead colors. Do the same with the lines, finding 15's for thin lines and 8's for thicker lines. As you plan your design, consider several factors: Are the printed shapes smaller than a single bead? Can shapes be made by grouping beads together? Which shapes are large enough to be outlined and then filled in with beads?

## Backstitch

**2.** Beginning with the largest shape, secure a thread by tying a tailor's knot in the back of the tie and pass through to the front along the outer edge of a paisley. Work backstitch (see Step 3, page 47), using 4 size 8's per stitch, following the main outline **(Figure 1)**. When you reach the start of the line, string just enough beads to reach the first bead without the beads buckling. Pass through the entire line of beads to help align them, then pass to the back and tie a knot to secure the thread.

**3.** Pass to the front, next to the outside of the beaded line. Backstitch size 11's all around. Finish by passing through the beads to align them, then secure the thread at the back and then pass through to the front inside the paisley.

Figure 1

*Getting Started with Seed Beads*

## Spangling

**4.** String 1 sequin and 1 bead. Slide the sequin down to the fabric and use the tip of the needle to help position it, then pass back through it to the back. Pull and hold the thread snug as you pass up at the edge of the sequin even with the bead at the center **(Figure 2)**. Repeat all around inside the beaded line, overlapping the sequins to conceal the fabric below or leaving space between them to show some extra color as you prefer.

## Center

**5.** Backstitch a mini paisley along the inner edge of the sequins using size 11°s.

**6.** To fill the mini paisley with stacked beads, string 1 size 8° and 1 size 15°. Pass back through the size 8° to the back, pull snug, and pass up next to the size 8° bead. Repeat, stacking and stitching beads in any space big enough for a size 8° **(Figure 3)**. To fill smaller spaces, simply string a single bead and pass back through the fabric.

## Finish your paisley

**7.** Secure the thread in the back of the fabric with a few knots and trim, or continue on to the next paisley until the whole tie is beaded.

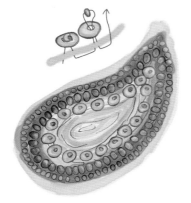

Figure 2

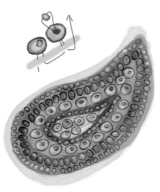

Figure 3

Ties aren't your thing? Turn your beaded motif into a brooch by adding a backing with a pin back finished with a beaded picot edge.

**Materials**

- Size 6° (A) and 8° (B) beads
- Beaded fabric
- Stiff felt backing
- 1" (2 cm) pin back
- Beading needle and thread

1. Cut the fabric ¼" (6 mm) all around the beads. Fold the fabric under along the outer row of beads.

2. Cut the felt to the same size and shape of the beadwork. Hold the pin back in place and cut two small slits at each end. Work the pin back through the slits to cover the bar **(Figure 1)**. Tie a knot at the end of 5' (1.5 m) of thread and secure the pin bar with a few stitches on the inside of the felt.

3. Place the beadwork on the felt and pass through both layers to secure the center with a few small stitches. Work the thread toward the edge.

4. Exit the back of the felt ⅛" (3 mm) from the edge. String 1A, 1B, and 1A and pass through the front of the beadwork to exit the felt about 1 bead's width away **(Figure 2)**. Pull snug and pass back through the last bead, forming a picot with 1 bead sticking up **(Figure 3)**.

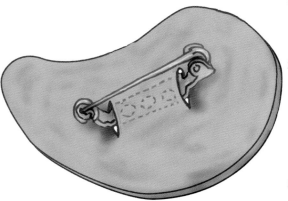

Figure 1

Figure 2

**5.** String 1B and 1A and pass front to back to exit 1 bead's width away from the last stitch; pull snug and pass back through the last bead. Repeat all around the edge, being sure that the fabric is tucked under and keeping the stitches just close enough that the beads touch (**Figure 4**). When you reach the first picot, string 1B and pass down through the first bead and through the front to the back (**Figure 5**). Pass up through the first bead and back through the last bead and down through the previous bead. Pass under the felt at the back to tie a knot around one of the edge stitches; repeat once, then trim.

Figure 3

Figure 4

Figure 5

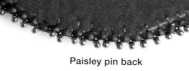

Paisley pin back

# 5

# Wired and Loopy

**Think "balloon animals" and you are well on your way to working with beaded wire.**

Make simple beaded sculptures by twisting, looping, and bending beaded wire. Colored wire will complement your beads where it peeks through.

Be careful to not kink the wire; even after straightening a kinked wire, it could break while you are working or, worse, after you are finished. Keep it smooth by gently drawing it between your thumb and fingers. You may straighten really bumpy wire with nylon-jaw pliers. Go easy with the pliers, as the wire hardens and becomes more brittle the more times you straighten it.

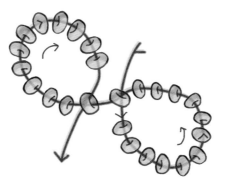

Wire can be used like thread to create sculptural shapes.

# Trillium Flower Scrunchies

## Materials

Size 6° seed beads for flower center (A)

Size 8° seed beads for petal base (B)
and petal (C)

26-gauge craft wire, 16" (41 cm) per
flower

Wire cutters

Round-nose pliers

Ponytail elastic

Use the wire as if it were thread to string beads, then pass through the first bead again to form each petal. Gather the petals to form a three-petal trillium flower with a layer of three additional petals or leaves below. Attach the flower to a hair band to put some spring in your step.

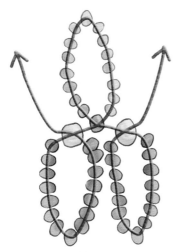

Figure 1

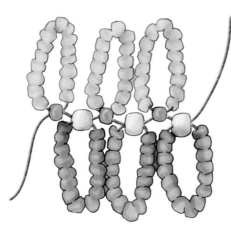

Figure 2

## Petals

**1.** Use 16" (41 cm) of wire to string 17C and slide them to the center of the wire. Use one end of the wire to string 1A, then pass the other end of the wire back through it. Gently pull the ends in opposite directions to snug the beads, forming a petal loop.

*Petal 2:* Use one end of the wire to string 1B and 17C. Slide the beads down to the base of the previous petal and hold them in place as you pass through the 1B again, then gently snug the beads to form another petal.

*Petal 3:* String 1A and 17C. Slide the beads down to the base of the previous petal and hold them in place as you pass through the 1A again, then gently snug the beads to form another petal **(Figure 1)**.

*Petals 4–6:* Use the other end of the wire to make three petals on the other side of the first petal, repeating from Petal 2 **(Figure 2)**.

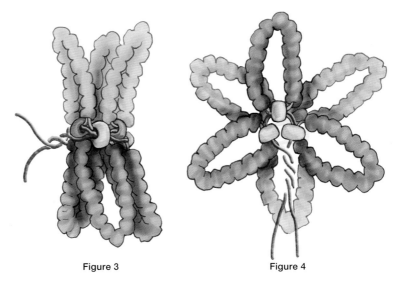

Figure 3                    Figure 4

## Twist and bloom

**2.** Pass one end of the wire through the first and second A at the other end of the petals, then pull the end of the wire to snug the petals into a bundle **(Figure 3)**. Pinch the bases of the petals together, with the larger size 6°s to the bottom and the size 8°s on top, then twist the wires tightly together a few times to secure. Arrange the petals in a flower shape **(Figure 4)**.

## Scrunchie

**3.** Lay the flower facedown with the twisted wire at the bottom. Pass both ends of the wire through the elastic and the top petal **(Figure 5)**. Pull the ends away from each other, snug inside the base of the petal, then around each side between the flower and the elastic, back toward the twist **(Figure 6)**.

**4.** Twist the ends together to secure, then pinch the elastic and wrap the wire around it a few times to hold it away from the flower. Trim the twisted wire to ½" (1 cm) and tuck the ends up into the base of the flower using round-nose pliers.

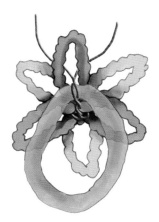

Figure 5

Figure 6

Instead of attaching these to hair elastics, you could dress up bobby pins, as shown here, by bending the wire around the flat side.

# Blooming Button Magnets

Wired bugle beads in bright colors go well with vintage buttons, giving them a modern look. Backed with a magnet, they'll bring cheer to your morning orange juice on even the gloomiest of days.

## Materials

Size 8° seed beads (for flower center)

Size 11°s and/or bugle beads (for petals)

1" (2.5 cm) shank button

1" (2.5 cm) magnet

26-gauge craft wire, 16" (41 cm) or more per flower

Wire cutters

Round-nose pliers

E-6000 cement

Toothpick

**1.** Cut 16" (41 cm) of wire from the spool. String about 3" (7.5 cm) of bugle beads and slide them to the center of the wire. Use one end of the wire to string 1 seed bead, then pass the other end of the wire back through it. Gently pull the ends in opposite directions to snug the beads, forming a petal loop.

**2.** For the second petal, string 1 seed bead and 3" (8 cm) of bugle beads; slide the beads down to the base of the previous petal and hold them in place as you pass through the 1 seed bead again; gently snug the beads to form another petal **(Figure 1)**. Repeat this step to make several more petals on each side of the first petal. As you work, arrange the petals in a circle and measure it against the button; the seed beads should fit around the shank on the back but be covered by the button in the front.

**3.** Pass one end of the wire through the first and second seed beads at the other end of the petals; pull the end of the wire to snug the petals into a circle. Work the wire through the shank of the button, weaving it through the petals if necessary to keep them secure and flat against the back of the button **(Figure 2)**.

**4.** Apply a generous amount of cement around the button shank and use the toothpick to work cement into the wires. Press the magnet into place, scraping excess cement off with the toothpick. Lay the flower on a junky towel and pile a couple books on top to keep things in place while the cement dries.

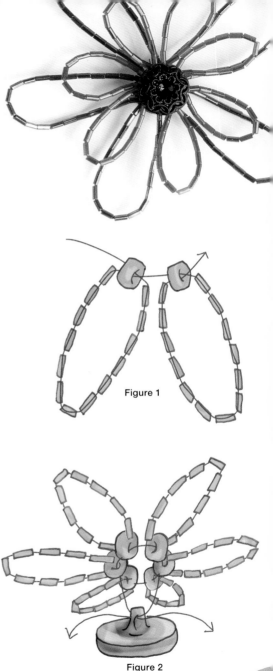

Figure 1

Figure 2

# 6 Netting

From ancient mummy shrouds to Victorian lampshades, netted beads have cast their sparkle upon many cultures and functions. Flexible in design and structure, netting can be used to quickly cover objects, including yourself.

Netting is often worked off the edge of a beaded trim or other foundation. Increases are easy to make because the lacy structure allows each row to expand or contract, adapting to the shape of the object underneath. Simply increase the number of beads that are strung between the shared beads of each unit.

Netting stitches can be easily manipulated to get dramatically different-looking structures. A row of single nets gives you a zigzag ribbon, two or more rows a lattice of diamonds. Sample a variation on netting, chevron stitch, which resembles a series of triangles and Vs.

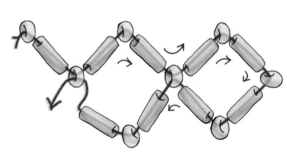

Single row of netting

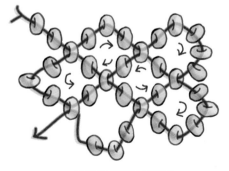

Adding rows in netting

# Curved Chevron Choker

## Materials

Size 6° red (A) and blue (B) seed
  beads
Size 8° cubes (C)
Size 11° striped blue (D) and
  metallic blue (F) seed beads

Size 8° ruby (E) seed beads
2 size 2° accent beads
1' (30.5 cm) of ¼" (6 mm) satin
  ribbon
Beading needle and thread

Make this netted chain by working a series of loops connected by
chevron nets that zigzag between
shared beads. The bottom loops
are worked with alternating colors
and are larger than the top loops,
causing the netting to curve.

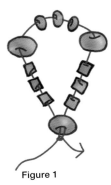

Figure 1

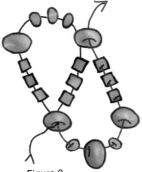

Figure 2

## Chevron chain

**1.** Use 6' (1.8 m) of thread to string 1A, 3C, 1A, 3D, 1A, and 3C, leaving a 4" (10 cm) tail. Pass back through the first 1A and tie a secure knot with the tail thread **(Figure 1)**.

*Blue bottom loop:* String 1D, 1B, 1D, 1A, and 3C; pass back through the second 1A of the previous loop and pull snug **(Figure 2)**.

*Top loop 1:* String 3D, 1A, and 3C; pass back through the 1A of the previous loop **(Figure 3)**.

*Red bottom loop:* String 2D, 1E, 2D, 1A, and 3C; pass back through the 1A of the previous loop **(Figure 4)**.

*Top loop 2:* Repeat Top Loop 1.

Repeat loop sequence to work about 9" (23 cm) of netted chain.

**2.** Reinforce the end of the chain by weaving through the beads of the last two loops, then pass back through the 3D of the last top loop. For a smooth edge, string 1F and pass back through the next 3D of the next net; repeat to add 1F between each top loop **(Figure 5a)**. Pass through the first two nets to reinforce, then tie a knot with the tail thread; secure the threads and trim.

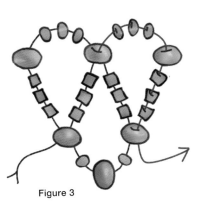

Figure 3

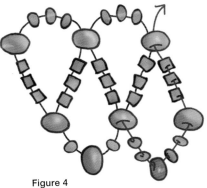

Figure 4

*Getting Started with Seed Beads*

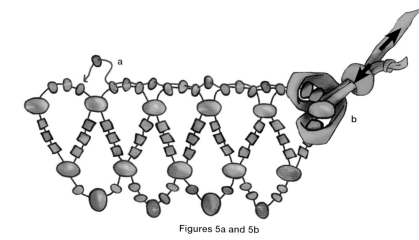

Figures 5a and 5b

## Clasp

**3.** Cut two 6" (15 cm) pieces of ribbon for the clasp. Tie an overhand knot at one end of a ribbon. Fold the ribbon near the knot and pass the fold through a size 2° bead to form a loop. Wrap the loop through one end of the chevron chain, then pass the bead and other end of the ribbon through the loop. Pull the ribbon to snug the knot up to the bead and the bead to the chain **(Figure 5b)**. String 1 size 8° onto the other end of the ribbon and tie an overhand knot to secure the bead. Repeat with the other ribbon for the other end of the chain.

# Green Diamond Ribbonette

This sequence creates a chain with double diamonds between even loops. Add a button and loop closure for a bracelet, or work a chain long enough for a lariat or belt.

**Materials**

Size 8° brass (A) and blue (B) seed beads

Size 11° silver-lined green (C) and matte green (D) seed beads

Size 15° brass (E) seed beads

Beading needle and thread

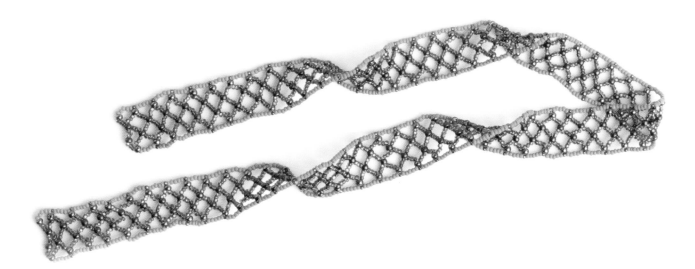

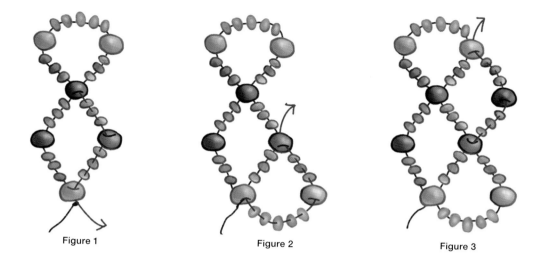

Figure 1          Figure 2          Figure 3

**1.** Use 6' of thread to string 1A, 3C, 1B, 3C, 1B, 3C, and 1A, leaving a 4"
tail. String 5D, 1A, and 3C; pass back through the last 1B. String 3C,
1B, and 3C; pass back through the first 1A and tie a knot with the tail
thread **(Figure 1)**.

*Bottom loop:* String 5D, 1A, and 3C; pass back through the last 1B
**(Figure 2)**. String 3C, 1B, and 3C; pass back through the top 1A
**(Figure 3)**.

*Top loop:* String 5D, 1A, and 3C; pass back through the last 1B. String
3C, 1B, and 3C; pass back through the bottom 1A.

**2.** Continue working Top and Bottom Loops for the desired length. To
reinforce the edges and straighten the ribbon, pass back through 5B,
string 1E, and pass back through the next 5B **(Figure 4)**.

Figure 4

# Spider Orbs

Prettier than cobwebs, and faster to make, these sparklies may quickly infest all the sun-filled windows or lampshades in your house, providing glints of color with mesmerizing spirals of pattern and turning some arachnids green with envy.

## Materials

Size 11° seed beads (A)

Size 2° bugle beads (B)

Size 8° seed beads (C)

2" (5 cm) glass ornament

Beading needle and thread

**1. *Foundation round:*** Use 6' (2 m) of thread to string 1A and 1B eight times, leaving a 6" (15 cm) tail. Pass through all the beads again to form a circle. Check that the circle fits around the top of the ornament; if necessary, rework the circle, adding seed beads between the bugle beads to increase. Tie a knot with the tail thread and pass through the next 1A.

**2. *Round 1:*** String 1B, 1A, and 1B; pass through the next 1A of the previous round. Repeat around to make 8 nets. After passing through the last 1A of the previous round, continue through the first 1B and 1A strung in this round.

***Round 2:*** String 1A, 1B, 3A, 1B, and 1A; pass through the 1A at the point of the next net in the previous round. Repeat around. Step up for the next round by passing through the first 4 beads strung in this round.

Round 1

Round 2

***Round 3:*** String 1A, 1B, 1A, 1C, 1A, 1B, and 1A; pass through the middle bead of the next net. Repeat around, then step up by passing through half of the first net of this round, exiting from the middle bead.

***Round 4:*** Repeat Round 3, stringing 1A, 1B, 1A, 1B, 1A, 1C, 1A, 1B, 1A, 1B, and 1A.

***Round 5:*** Repeat Round 4, stringing 2A, 1C, and 2A for the center of each net.

***Round 6:*** Work fringes in this round. String 3A, 1B, 1A, 1B, 1A, 1B, 2A, 1C, 2A, 1B, 1A, 1B, 2A, 1C, and 1A. Snug the beads and, skipping the last bead, pass back through beads to the first 1C just strung. String 2A, 1B, 1A, 1B, 1A, 1B, and 3A; pass through the 1C of the next net in the previous row. Repeat around for a total of 8 fringes.

**3.** To finish, weave through several nets, tying knot between beads, and trim close. Use the tail thread to reinforce the first round, then trim close.

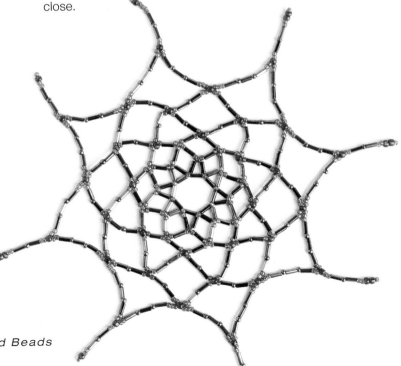

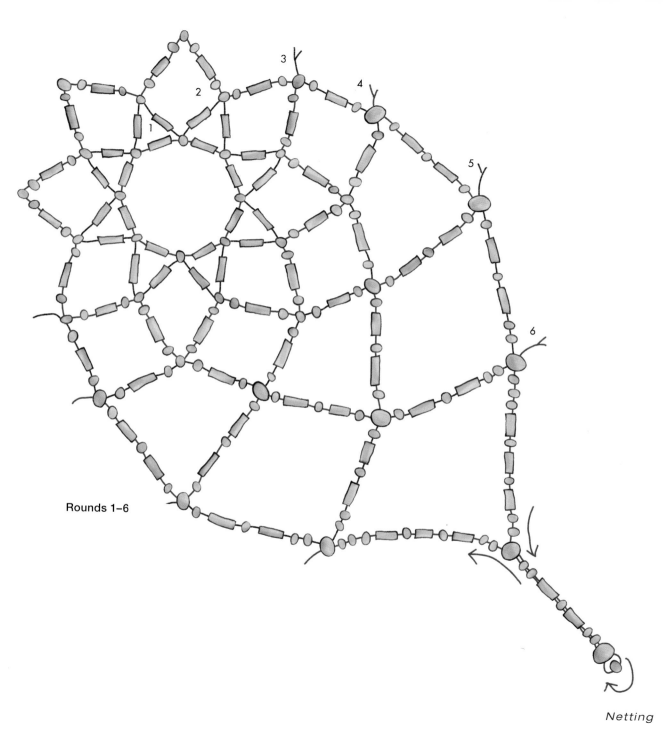

Rounds 1–6

# 7

# Peyote Stitches

A popular stitch, peyote is often used for flat, charted images, or worked in the round to make trinket-size bags. It can go "off the charts" to create sculptural objects, thanks to its inter-locking bead structure. It works up fast because each bead is passed through only twice—once when you string it and once when securing a bead of the next row.

Peyote stitch begins with stringing the first two rows at once, alternating one bead from each row. The third row is worked by stitching each bead between two beads of the second row, so that it rests on top of a bead in the first row.

Because the beads are staggered (one half up, the next half down), each row really consists of only half the total bead width; for instance, a peyote-stitched strip that is 6 beads wide has 3 beads per worked row.

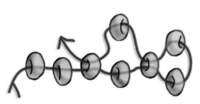

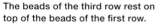

The beads of the third row rest on top of the beads of the first row.

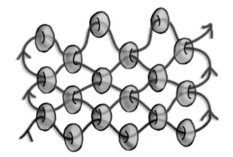

A strip 6 beads wide contains 3 beads per row.

## Odd-count flat peyote

When a row ends with an even number of beads, simply flip your work over, string the first bead of the next row, and you're good to go.

Odd-count peyote stitch allows you to work patterns not possible with even-count, like diamonds or Vs that end in a single-bead point. The drawback is that you have to do some fancy needlework. An odd ending to a row means that there is no spot available for the next bead, resulting in the "odd-count turn," which you will learn on page 79.

**Odd count**      **Even count**

## Tubular peyote

If the first two rows of peyote stitch are a circle of beads, then you can go round and round, making tubular peyote. Even-count tubular peyote stitch requires a step up at the end of each round—that is, passing through the first bead of the round just worked—in order to be in place for the next round. Odd-count tubular peyote stitch does not require a step up; simply continue around, stringing a bead between each pair of up beads. The color pattern is determined in the foundation round and forms a spiral.

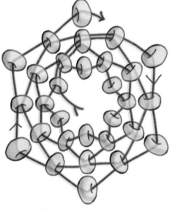

**Tubular peyote stitch**

# Snappy Bands

To make these fun bracelets, work a strip of beadwork using size 6° beads in alternating colors for each row. Using two colors creates stripes of each color and helps show you where to stitch when starting the first rows. The two alternative edges not only add decorative flair to an otherwise flat bracelet but also help protect the exposed thread and extend the life of your band.

## Materials

Size 6° seed beads for
  base strip (A and B)
Size 11° seed beads for
  edging (C and D)

Sew-on snap
Needle and thread

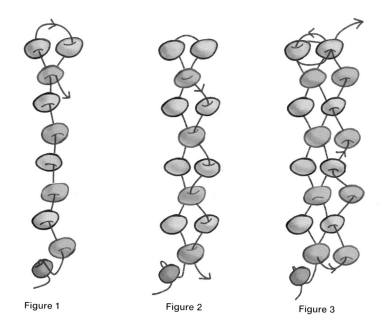

Figure 1          Figure 2          Figure 3

## Peyote strip

**1.** Use 6' (1.8 m) to string 1 bead and pass through it again to form a tension bead, leaving an 8" (20.5 cm) tail.

*Rows 1 and 2:* For an 8-bead-wide strip, begin by stringing 1 bead and passing through it again to form a tension bead, leaving an 8" tail. String 1A and 1B four times (8 beads total); slide them down to the tension bead.

*Row 3:* String 1B and pass back through the last 1A. Pull the thread snug so that the 2Bs sit side by side and the other beads are snug to the tension bead **(Figure 1)**. String 1B and pass back through the next 1A, and pull snug. Repeat twice more **(Figure 2)**.

*Row 4:* String 1A and pass back through the last 1B. String 1A and pass back through the next 1B; repeat twice. Secure the row by passing through the 2 edge beads **(Figure 3)**.

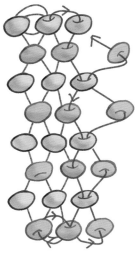

Figure 4

Repeat Rows 3 and 4, securing each row by passing through 2 edge beads before starting the next row **(Figure 4)**. Stop beading when the strip fits comfortably around your wrist with a ³/₄" (2 cm) overlap (about 7¹/₂" [19 cm] total length).

**2.** To fill the jagged edge of the last row, string 2 size 11°s to stitch between each of the 6° beads sticking up in the previous row **(Figure 5a)**. Pass through the last two rows once more to reinforce.

**Snap**

**3.** Pass through the beads to exit the center of the third-to-last row, and string one half of the snap **(Figure 5b)**. Weave through neighboring beads to pass through each hole of the snap several times to secure. Remove the tension bead and use the tail thread to work 1 row of size 11°s at the other end of the strip; attach the other half of the snap, being sure to sew it onto the opposite side of the strip. Secure the threads and trim.

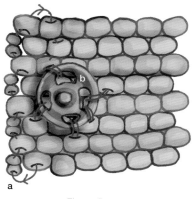

Figure 5

*Getting Started with Seed Beads*

## Edging

**4.** Secure a new thread and exit from an edge bead at one end of the strip to work one of the following beaded edgings with size 11°s to protect the exposed peyote-stitched thread along the sides of the strip.

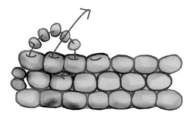

Figure 6

### Roped edge

Create a smooth braided look with a series of overlapping loops.

***Loop 1:*** String 5C, skip 1 edge bead, and pass down through the third edge bead. Pass up through the second edge bead, passing the needle behind the 5-bead loop just strung; pull snug **(Figure 6)**.

***Loop 2:*** String 5D, skip 1 edge bead and pass down through the following edge bead; pass up through the skipped edge bead, coming up behind the 5-bead loop just strung; pull snug **(Figure 7)**.

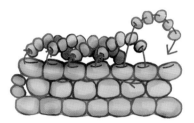

Figure 7

Continue for the length of the bracelet, alternating loops of 5C and 5D and always bringing the needle up behind the loop with each stitch. Pass through the last peyote-stitched row to repeat on the opposite edge.

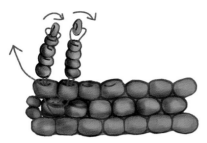

Figure 8

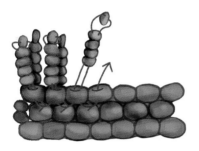

Figure 9

**Fringes**

This feathery trim yields 2 different fringes from each edge bead.

***Fringe Set 1:*** String 5C and slide them down to the work. Hold the thread and beads taut while you pass back through the first 4C and the edge bead below it; pull snug, tugging on the fifth bead if necessary to take up the slack in the thread. Pass up through the next edge bead and string 5C to work a second fringe **(Figure 8)**.

***Fringe Set 2:*** Pass up through the first edge bead again. String 4D and pass back through the first 3D to work a second fringe off the same bead. Repeat for the second edge bead **(Figure 9)**.

Pass up through the next empty edge bead to continue, repeating Sets 1 and 2 for both edges of the bracelet.

# Beaded Cylinder Beads

## Materials

Size 11° seed beads in 3 shades of one color, plus 1 accent color (A, B, C, D)
Needle and thread

Each cylinder is worked as a flat strip that alternates three colors of 2-bead stitches, with 1-bead stitches of the accent color between them, then the ends are "zipped" together to form a tube. The tubes make great beaded beads when strung together on a ribbon, or a single tube can be used as a beaded toggle, as seen in the Supple Tiles Necklace on page 106.

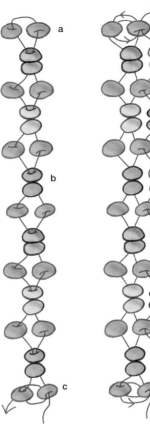

Figure 1

Figure 2

## Peyote strip

**1.** Use 4' (1 m) of thread to string 2D; pass through them again leaving a 4" (10 cm) tail, then pass through the first bead again. (These beads will act as a tension bead, but will become part of the work rather than being removed.)

*Rows 1 and 2:* String 2A, 1D, 2B, 1D, 2C, 1D, 2A, 1D, 2B, 1D, 2C, and 1D.

*Row 3:* String 1D and pass back through the last 2C; pull snug so that the 2D sit side by side **(Figure 1a)**. String 1D and pass back through the next 2B. String 1D and pass back through the next 2A. Continue, stitching 1D between each 2-bead set of the previous row **(Figure 1b)**. After passing through the last 2 beads, pass through the 2D to exit from the opposite side of the tail thread **(Figure 1c)**.

*Row 4:* String 2B and pass through the next 1D. String 2C and pass through the next 1D. Repeat, stringing 2A, then 2B, then 2C, then 2A. Secure the end of the row by passing through the 2 edge beads previously worked **(Figure 2)**.

***Row 5:*** String 1D and pass back through the last 2-bead set **(Figure 3a)**; repeat for the length of Row 5. To make an odd-count turn, string 1D and pass through the previous edge bead and the previous 2-bead set; pull snug, then pass through the last 2-bead set, the previous edge bead, and the last 1D just strung **(Figure 3b)**.

***Row 6:*** String 2C and pass back through the next 1D. Repeat, stringing 2A, then 2B, then 2C, then 2A, then 2B. Secure the end of the row by passing through the 2 edge beads.

***Row 7:*** Repeat Row 5.

***Row 8:*** Repeat Row 6, beginning with 2A.

***Row 9:*** Repeat Row 5.

***Row 10:*** Repeat Row 6, beginning with 2B.

***Row 11:*** Repeat Row 5.

***Row 12:*** Repeat Row 6, beginning with 2C.

***Rows 13–18:*** Repeat Rows 7–12.

For the large tubes shown in the sample bracelet, repeat Rows 7–12 again for a total of 24 rows.

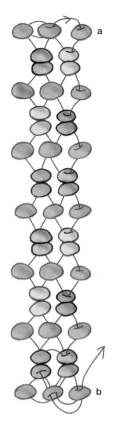

Figure 3

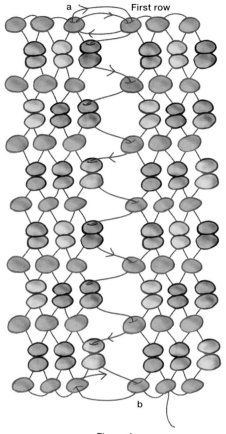

a

First row

b

Figure 4

## Zipping up

**2.** When you work an even number of rows, the first and last rows will fit together like the teeth of a zipper. Pass through the first row and last row edge beads twice and pull snug to secure the end of the last row **(Figure 4a)**. Stitch back through the last and first rows, zipping them together, and pass through the edge beads several times at the other end **(Figure 4b)**. Secure the thread by passing back through several beads. Do the same with the tail thread, then trim the threads close to the work.

# Spiral Tubes

## Materials

Size 8° seed beads in green, blue, and bronze/red

Needle and thread

Chopstick and tape (optional)

These ropy tubes have two colors that form stripes, accented with a third color that highlights the spiral created by working in the round. With size 8° beads, they work up fast enough to make a choker length necklace or doubled bangle with a hidden snap closure. To help you past the first few rounds you can use a pencil or chopstick to keep the beads in order. Sample both the even- and odd-count methods to see how the spirals develop.

Figure 1

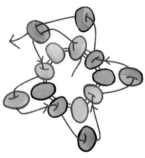

Figure 2

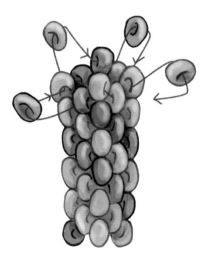

Figure 3

## Odd-count tube

***Rounds 1 and 2:*** Use 6' (2 m) of thread to string 1 green, 2 bronze, 2 blue, 2 green, and 2 blue. Pass through all the beads again, leaving an 8" (20 cm) tail, and pull tight to form a circle. Pass through the first green again **(Figure 1)**. Place the ring onto the chopstick, pointed end up, and tape the tail below toward the handle.

***Round 3:*** String 1 green, skip 1 bead, and pass through the following bead in the previous round (bronze). String 1 bronze, skip 1 bead, and pass through the following bead (blue). String 1 blue, skip 1 bead, and pass through the following bead (green). String 1 green, skip 1 bead, and pass through the following bead (blue). String 1 blue, skip 1 bead, and pass through the following bead, the first green in this round **(Figure 2)**.

***Rounds 4 and on:*** Repeat Round 3; for each stitch string the same color as the bead just passed through, then pass through the next "up bead" **(Figure 3)**. Remove the chopstick after working a few rounds. Continue until the piece measures about 16" (41 cm).

## Snap

Attach half of the snap to the end of the tube—string 1 hole of the snap, then pass through the next 2 beads, up through the next hole of the snap, and pull snug. Repeat around twice more, passing down through 2 or 3 beads with each stitch to reinforce. Weave back through a few rounds to secure the thread and trim close. Repeat to attach the other half of the snap using the tail thread.

## Even-count tube

*Rounds 1 and 2:* Use 6' (2 m) of thread to string 2 red, then 1 blue and 1 green eight times (10 beads total). Pass through all the beads again, leaving an 8" (20.5 cm) tail, and pull tight to form a circle. Place the ring onto the chopstick, pointed end up, and tape the tail below toward the handle. Pass through the first 2 red again **(Figure 4)**.

*Round 3:* String 1 red and pass through the next green. String 1 blue and pass through the next green; repeat three times, arriving at the 2 red again. String 1 blue for the fifth and final bead of this round and pass through 2 red (the last bead in the previous round and the first bead strung in this round) to step up **(Figure 5)**.

*Round 4:* String 1 red and pass through the next blue. String 1 green and pass through the next blue; repeat three times. String 1 green for the fifth and final bead of this round and pass through 2 red to step up **(Figure 6)**.

**TIP:** To keep track of when you need to step up, start each round with a contrasting color. You will see how the start of each round shifts position by one bead, evidenced by the contrasting spiral.

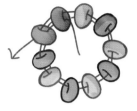

Figure 4

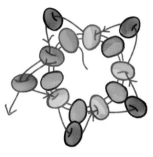

Figure 5

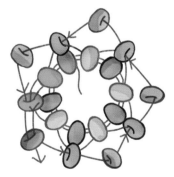

Figure 6

**Rounds 5 and on:** Repeat Rounds 3 and 4 until the tube measures about 16" (40.5 cm) **(Figure 7)**.

### Snap

Work 2 size 11°s in each stitch to even the jagged edge, then attach a snap as with the odd-count tube.

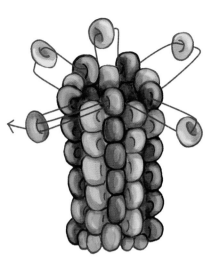

Figure 7

Even-count peyote tube

Odd-count peyote tube

# Ladders and Angles

The single-needle version of ladder stitch is a pass-through stitch—the thread always travels through the beads in the same direction, looping in a figure-eight pattern.

Right-angle weave shares the same thread path as ladder stitch, with the addition of one or more beads on each side of the connecting beads, forming a 4-sided unit. Each unit shares the connecting beads of the units before and after it to form a chain. In the double-needle versions, two threads cross in opposite directions through each connecting bead.

Mostly used to form a foundation row for other stitches, ladder stitch connects one or more beads to an equal number of beads, stacking them side by side, with exposed thread and holes along each edge.

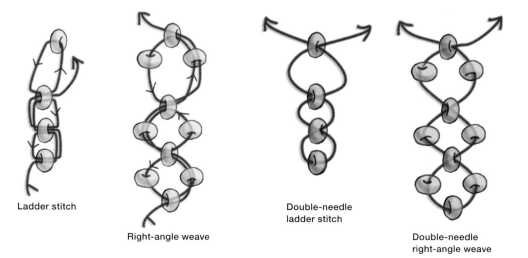

Ladder stitch

Right-angle weave

Double-needle ladder stitch

Double-needle right-angle weave

# Ladder Rings

Make a ladder of 2-bead stacks, then join the ends to form a ring. Add beads along each side of the ladder to embellish and finish the edges. When you're comfortable with the technique, follow the directions on page 88 to make a coordinating bracelet of linked ladder bands.

directions on page 88

## Materials

Size 8° and 11° seed beads

Needle and thread

*Getting Started with Seed Beads*

## Ladder band

**1.** Use 4' (1.3 m) of thread to string 4 size 8°s and pass through them again, leaving a 4" (10 cm) tail. Arrange the beads side by side to form two 2-bead stacks, holding the tail at the bottom and to the left **(Figure 1)**.

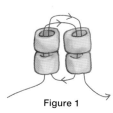

Figure 1

**2.** String 2 beads and pass down through the last 2 beads passed through. Pull snug, then pass up through the 2 beads just strung. String 2 beads and pass up through the last 2 beads passed through. Pull snug, then pass down through the 2 beads just strung **(Figure 2)**. Repeat, stringing 2 beads for each stitch, and alternate working clockwise and counter-clockwise.

Figure 2

**3.** Stop adding beads when the ladder is long enough to wrap around your finger and has an even number of stacks. Connect the ends of the ladder by passing through the first and last 2-bead stacks **(Figure 3)**.

Figure 3

## Edging

**4.** String 2 size 11°s and pass through the next stack to exit the other side of the ladder; repeat around the ring **(Figure 4)**. When you reach the point where you started, string 2 size 11°s and pass through the next stack in the opposite direction; repeat to add 2 beads between each of the 2 beads just worked. Pass through all the size 11°s on one side of the ladder to reinforce and snug the beads, then pass through the ladder and reinforce the beads on the other side in the same way **(Figure 5)**. Pass through both edges as many times as the holes will allow without breaking any beads, then trim the thread close.

Figure 4

**5. Embellishing (optional):** Pass through edge beads and connect them with bars of smaller beads to add another layer (or two!) around the ring as in the silver ring at left.

Figure 5

# Linked Ladder Bracelet

When you're hooked on little ladder rings, join them together to form a bracelet—or go wild and made enough for a necklace.

**Materials**

About 20 Ladder Rings, half with ends not joined

Sew-on snap

Beading needle and thread

1. Link rings by making a ladder band and passing it through a previous ring before connecting its ends. Continue until the chain nearly reaches around your wrist.

2. For a clasp link, make one ladder about ¼" (6 mm) longer than the other links. Without joining the ends, work beads along both edges to match the links. Stitch one end of this ladder to the edge of the last chain link; at the same time, stitch one half of a snap to the inside of the link (**Figure 1a**). Stitch through the edges and snap several times to secure.

3. Pass through beads to exit near the other end of the ladder. Check the fit of the chain, then stitch the other half of the snap securely to the ladder (**Figure 1b**). Weave in the thread and tail and trim close.

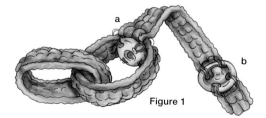

Figure 1

# Right-angle Bangle

Use two needles to work a simple right-angle chain, then embellish it with a crisscross of beads for a luxurious rounded rope. With the ends joined to make a bangle, you can easily roll it on over your knuckles and start the next one! Make one long enough to fit over your heel, and you'll have a right-angle ankle bangle.

## Materials

Size 6°, 8°, and 11° seed beads (A, B, C)

Two needles and thread

## Right-angle base

**1.** To start a chain of 4-bead units using two-needle right-angle weave, cut 5' (1.5 m) of thread and place a needle on each end.

Figure 1

*First unit:* Use one needle to string 4A and slide them to the center of the thread; with the other needle, pass back through the last bead strung and pull the needles in opposite directions to snug the beads **(Figure 1)**.

*Following units:* *Use the left needle to string 2A; pinch the second bead between your thumb and finger, letting the needle fall to the palm of your hand. Use the right needle to string 1A and pass back through the pinched bead **(Figure 2)**. Repeat from * to add units until the chain is 7" (18 cm), or long enough to fit around your closed hand **(Figure 3)**.

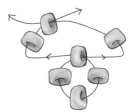

Figure 2

### Using two needles

When you pass back through a strung bead, the needle might pierce the thread inside it, weakening the thread and preventing it from sliding through the bead. When this happens, you must remove the needle, pull the thread loose, and rethread the needle. To avoid that hassle, develop the following habit for working two-needle right-angle weave:

- Use the left needle to string 2 beads. Pull the needle through the beads and drop it into your palm, pinching the thread tight under the beads.
- Use the right needle to string 1 bead and pass back through the last bead of the other needle (pinched in your fingers).
- Release the pinched beads and take the right needle with your left hand, grab the left needle with your right hand, and pull in opposite directions to snug the beads.

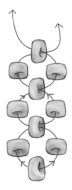

Figure 3

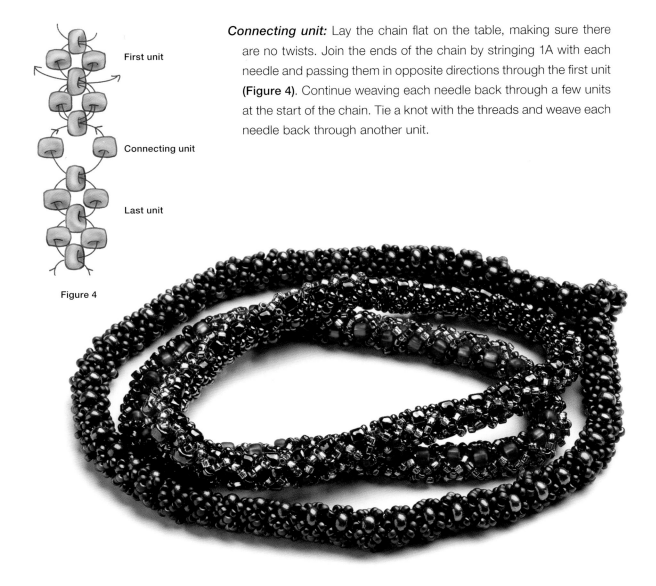

First unit

Connecting unit

Last unit

Figure 4

**Connecting unit:** Lay the chain flat on the table, making sure there are no twists. Join the ends of the chain by stringing 1A with each needle and passing them in opposite directions through the first unit **(Figure 4)**. Continue weaving each needle back through a few units at the start of the chain. Tie a knot with the threads and weave each needle back through another unit.

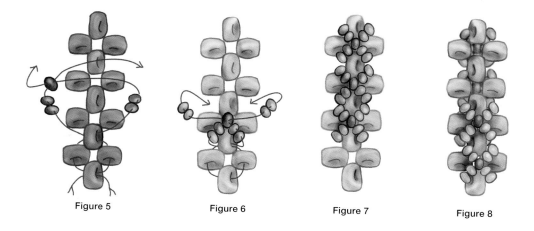

Figure 5     Figure 6     Figure 7     Figure 8

## Embellishing

**2.** Continue using two needles to add smaller beads on top of the chain, working 2 stitches to form an X on top of each base unit.

*Stitch 1:* Use the left needle to string 2C and 1B; pinch the 1B and let the needle fall to your palm. Use the right needle to string 2C and pass back through the 1B. Pull the needles in opposite directions to snug the beads **(Figure 5)**.

*Stitch 2:* Use each needle to string 2C and pass each one through the next size 6° of the chain, crossing the needles in opposite directions **(Figure 6)**.

**3.** Repeat Stitches 1 and 2 to make an X on top of each unit all around one side of the chain **(Figure 7)**.

**4.** When you reach the first X, turn the embellished side of the chain to the inside and work another round in different colors on the other side of each unit **(Figure 8)**. Finish the bangle by passing each thread through a few units, tying a knot with both threads, passing through a few beads, then trimming.

# 9 Brick Stitch

In brick stitch, the beads not only form an interlocking pattern, they also rely on thread to hold them together the way mortar holds a brick wall.

Unlike other stitches, brick stitch is worked off the thread that connects the beads of a previous row rather than the beads themselves.

A foundation is required before the first row of brick stitch can be laid, usually the exposed thread along the edges of ladder- or peyote-stitched beads. This is a "pass-back-through" stitch—each bead is secured to the thread below it, then passed back through to the top of the bead. Stringing the next bead forms a bridge of new thread along the top of the beads and provides the foundation for the next row.

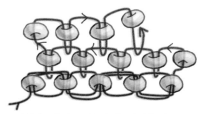

**Brick stitch worked off a ladder base.**

# Bricks and Strands Bracelet

## Materials

Size 11° seed beads in matte
   copper, gilt-lined rose, magenta,
   cobalt blue, and matte blue
Size 8° seed beads in metallic copper
5mm copper bugle beads

4mm copper cubes
15mm copper shank button
Needle and thread
Pencil and paper
Ruler

Make two brick-stitched triangles
that decrease to a button-and-loop
closure, then connect their bases
with strands of beads. Simple color
gradations contrast with strands
of bugle beads to add a change of
texture.

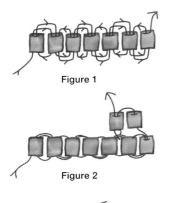

Figure 1

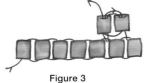

Figure 2

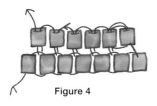

Figure 3

Figure 4

## Triangle Ends

**1.** Use cube beads and 6' (2 m) of thread to brick-stitch a triangle, beginning with a ladder-stitched base row:

*Ladder base:* String 2 cubes; pass through them again, leaving a 6" (15 cm) tail. String 1 cube and pass through the last cube and the cube just strung. Repeat four times to make a 7-bead ladder **(Figure 1)**.

*Row 1:* String 2 cubes and pass under the second-to-last loop of thread that connects the beads of the base row **(Figure 2)**. Snug the beads, then pass back through the last bead strung. Pass through both beads again to secure them at the start of the row **(Figure 3)**. String 1 cube and pass under the next loop of the previous row; snug the bead into place, then pass back through it. Repeat for the length of the row, stitching 1 bead for each loop of thread, 6 beads total **(Figure 4)**.

*Rows 2–4:* Flip your work over so the working thread is to the right to work the next row. Repeat Row 1 for a total of 5 beads. Flip again and work a 4-bead row, then again to work a 3-bead row **(Figure 5)**.

Repeat Step 1 to make a second triangle.

## Button

**2.** With the thread exiting an edge bead of the last row of one triangle, string 4 size 11°s, the button, 1 size 8°, and 1 size 11°; snug the beads, then pass back through the size 8° and button. String 4 size 11°s and pass down through the opposite edge bead. Reinforce the beads by passing down through the second bead of the previous row, up through the following and into the edge bead to pass through all the beads and button again **(Figure 6)**. Pass down through the edge beads along one side to exit the base of the triangle; set aside.

Figure 6

## Loop

**3.** Exiting an edge bead of the last row of the second triangle, string 1 size 8°, 24 size 11°s (or enough to fit snugly around the button), and 1 size 8°. Pass down through the opposite edge and pull snug. Check that the button fits through the loop and adjust if necessary. Weave through the brick-stitched rows in order to exit the size 8° and pass through the loop again to reinforce **(Figure 7)**.

Figure 7

**4.** *Embellish loop:* Exit the size 8° at the base of the loop. String 2 size 11°s and 1 size 8°; pass back through the next pair of loop beads, snug the beads and pass through the last bead strung **(Figure 8)**. Repeat around the outside of the loop, stitching 1 size 8° to each pair of size 11°s. Weave through beads to pass through the outer loop of beads again to reinforce, then pass down through beads along one edge of the triangle.

Figure 8

7"

Figure 9

## Strands

**5.** Use a piece of paper to help lay out your design. Mark the desired finished length (about 7") on the paper. Place the tip of a triangle at each mark, with the threads exiting at opposite corners. Divide the space between the triangles into seven equal sections and mark them on the paper.

**6.** Use one of the threads to string enough size 11°s to reach the other triangle, changing colors for each section. Pass up through the corresponding cube on the opposite triangle, string 1 size 11°, snug the beads, then pass back through the cube and the entire strand to pass up through the first cube and down through the following cube in the base row. Repeat with the other thread, so that you have one strand at each edge of the triangles **(Figure 9)**.

**7.** Check for size—if the fit is loose, work the following strands a little shorter to snug the fit; if tight, work strands slightly longer. Follow the paper guide to string each strand, varying the length of each color section slightly to create a gradated effect. Pass through corresponding cubes and up through beads to exit an edge cube, string 1 size 11°, then pass back through the cubes to the next cube of the base row.

**8.** Work a second set of strands so that each cube has two strands; work a few strands of bugle beads with size 8°s between each. Finish by weaving through cubes and then passing through a strand, tying half hitch knots, and trim close.

### Adding thread

When your thread is too short to work a whole strand, weave through a few cubes to pass back through some of a finished strand. Tie a half hitch knot and pass through a few beads; repeat to tie a few knots, then trim close. Begin a new thread by weaving through cubes to secure the tail, then tie a knot around a loop of thread along the triangle base.

*Getting Started with Seed Beads*

# Comet Tail Earrings

## Materials

Size 15° seed beads

2mm bugle beads

1.5mm cubes

Pair of ear wires

Needle and thread

Brick stitch can be worked with two beads in each stitch (called 2-drop), making each row two beads tall. Beginning with a ladder-stitched base row, use small cubes or cylinders to work tall triangles, then add fringe with bugle beads to give them sleek, flashy movement.

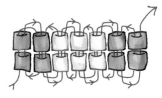

Figure 1

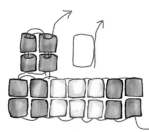

Figure 2

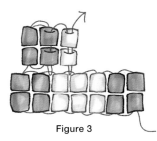

Figure 3

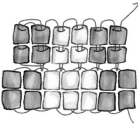

Figure 4

## Comet head

**1. Ladder base:** Use 5' (1.5 m) of thread to string 4 cubes and pass through them again, leaving a 4" (10 cm) tail. Pull snug so that you have two 2-bead stacks. String 2 cubes and pass through the last 2 cubes and the 2 just strung; repeat to make a 7-stack ladder **(Figure 1)**.

**Row 1:** String 4C cubes and pass under the second loop on top of the ladder; pull snug and pass back through the last 2C cubes. Pass through all 4C cubes again to secure the start of the row **(Figure 2)**. String 2C cubes and pass under the next loop; pull snug and pass back through the 2C cubes just strung **(Figure 3)**. Repeat for a total of six 2-bead stacks **(Figure 4)**.

**Rows 2–5:** Continue working 2 beads with each stitch, ending with a row of two 2-bead stacks.

*Getting Started with Seed Beads*

## Ear wire

**2.** String 7A and 1 ear wire and pass down through the opposite stack **(Figure 5)**. Snug the beads and pass through the loop of beads again to reinforce. Pass down through the beads along one edge of the triangle to exit the bottom of the base row.

## Comet tail

**3.** Work a set of graded fringe along the base of the triangle **(Figure 6)**.

*Fringe 1:* String 1A seed bead, 1B bugle, 1A seed, 1B bugle, 1C cube, and 1A seed. Snug the beads up to the triangle and hold the thread taut while you pass back through them, skipping the last bead strung. Pass up through the first stack and down through the next stack of the base row.

*Fringe 2:* String 1A seed and 1B bugle four times; string 1C cube and 1A seed. Make a fringe and pass down through the next stack.

*Fringe 3:* String 8A seeds, 1B bugle, 1A seed, 1B bugle, 1A seed, 1B bugle, 1A seed, 1B bugle, 1C cube, and 1A; make a fringe and pass down through the next stack.

*Fringe 4:* String 12A, 1B bugle, 1A seed, 1B bugle, 1A seed, 1B bugle, 1A seed, 1B bugle, 1C cube, and 1A; make a fringe and pass down through the next stack.

*Fringes 5–7:* Repeat Fringes 3–1.

**4.** Finish the earring by passing up through the edge beads and through the loop again; weave through beads to secure, then trim close.

Repeat from Step 1 to make a second earring.

Figure 5

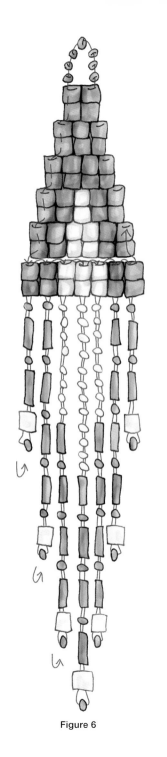

Figure 6

# Belted Bricky Balls

Ladder-stitched belts of bugle beads (held in place with tape) serve as the foundation for rounds of tubular brick stitch. Because brick stitch is worked off a foundation of thread instead of other beads, decreasing the tube to the shape of the wooden bead inside is easy. The final round uses a brick-stitch picot to finish around the hole. String one or more on a shoelace for a simply fun necklace.

## Materials

Size 11° (C) and 15° (A) seed beads

Size 2 bugle beads (B)

1" (2 cm) wood bead

¼" (6 mm) wide double-sided craft tape

Needle and thread

## Bugle bead

**1.** Use 6' (2 m) of thread to string 1A, 1B, 2A, 1B, and 1A; pass through all the beads again and pull snug so that you have two 3-bead stacks, then pass through them again to reinforce. String 1A, 1B, and 1A; pass down through the last 3-bead stack, pull snug, then pass up through the 3 beads just strung. Continue stringing 3 beads and passing in alternate directions for each stitch, until you have a strip that reaches nearly around the wood bead **(Figure 1)**.

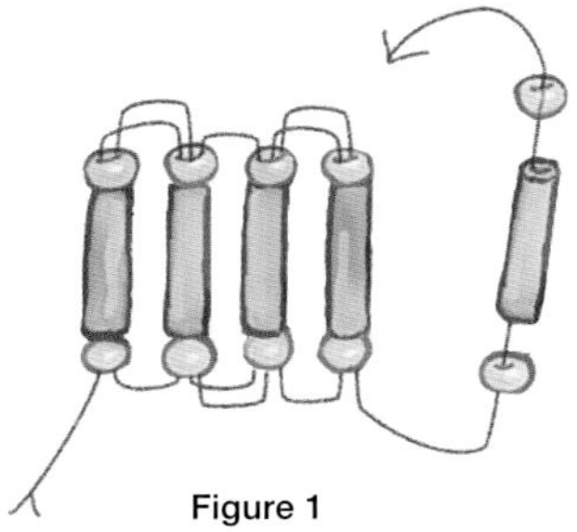

Figure 1

**2.** Wrap a narrow band of tape around the equator of the bead. Press the ladder to the tape all around, making sure the beads are even and snug. Work more stitches if needed to reach the first stitch, then pass through the first and last 3-bead stacks to connect the ends of the ladder, exiting from a size 15° **(Figure 2)**.

### Brick stitch

**3.** Work brick stitch with size 11°s to cover one side of the bead.

*Round 1:* String 2C and pass under the next loop of thread along the top of the ladder; pull snug, then pass back through the second bead just strung. String 1C and pass under the next loop, pull snug, and pass back through the bead; repeat all around. Finish the round by passing down through the first bead and up through the last bead of this round **(Figure 3)**.

*Rounds 2 and on:* Repeat Round 1, anchoring each stitch to the thread on top of the previous round and working decreases as necessary to keep the beads snug to the wooden bead. There is no set rule for when to make a decrease—simply pass under any loop that is between a half and a whole bead's width from the last bead worked. If there is a gap between the brick-stitched beads and the wood, work more decreases; if there are gaps between the seed beads, work fewer decreases. Cover the bead until you are one round away from the edge of the hole.

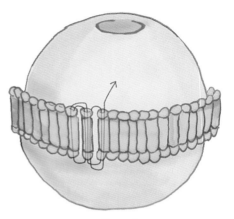

Figure 2

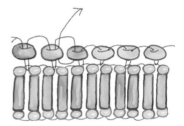

Figure 3

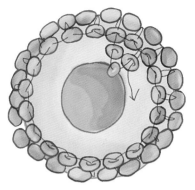

Figure 4

*Picot round:* String 1C, 1A, and 1C; pass under a loop of thread, pull snug, and pass back through the last bead strung **(Figure 4)**. String 1A and 1C, pass under a loop of thread and back through the last bead strung; repeat all around **(Figure 5)**. To finish the round, string 1A and pass down through the first 1C of the round and up through the last 1C. Pass through all the size 15° a few times to reinforce and snug them into a tight circle **(Figure 6)**.

**4.** Weave through beads to exit the other side of the ladder belt and repeat from Round 1 to work the other half of the bead. Secure the thread by weaving back through beads, then trim close.

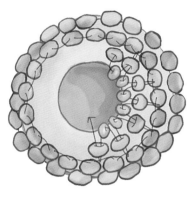

Figure 5

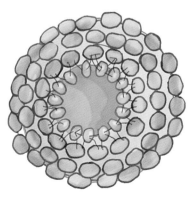

Figure 6

### Tips

- Bugle beads often have sharp edges that may rub against the thread, eventually cutting through it. This ladder-stitched belt of bugle beads uses size 15°s to protect the thread; their small diameter allows the bugle beads to be snug to each other, whereas size 11°s would cause gaps between the bugle beads.
- When brick-stitching a round of beads that are larger than the beads of the previous round, do not pass under every loop of thread. When stitching smaller beads on top of larger beads, you may pass under the same loop of thread more than once.
- To keep the brick-stitched beads snug to the wooden bead, work decreases by skipping a loop of thread whenever the distance to the next loop is shorter than the width of a bead.

*Getting Started with Seed Beads*

# Not-so-square Stitch

Square-stitched beads form a flexible grid, with each bead stitched one at a time to the bead below it. The thread travels in a loopy path, passing through each bead three times, creating a very strong piece of beaded fabric. Stitching 2 beads to a single bead in the previous row will create a curve.

Graphed motifs, such as cross-stitch designs, can be adapted for beading to make pictorial patterns, but keep in mind that most seed beads are taller than they are wide, distorting a square pattern into a tall rectangle.

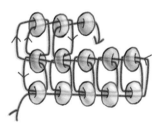

**Square stitch**

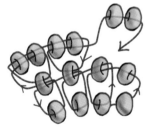

**Circular square stitch**

# Supple Tiles Necklace

Square stitch creates a cloth from glass. Connect squares of this cloth with strands of beads for a kinetic geometric collar. Practice working from a chart, then refresh your peyote skills with a beaded cylinder toggle.

### Materials

Size 8° hex beads in three colors (A, B, C)

Size 11° hex beads

Beading needle and thread

*Getting Started with Seed Beads*

## Tiles

Make 5 square-stitched tiles—1 large, 2 medium, and 2 small.

**1.** Begin each tile with 6' (2 m) of thread (4' [1 m] for the small tiles) and string a tension bead, leaving a 9" (23 cm) tail.

*Row 1:* Referring to the corresponding chart, string all of the beads for the first row, reading from left to right (15 beads for the large tile, 11 for medium, or 7 for the small tile).

*Row 2:* String the first bead of the second row and pass through the last bead of the previous row and the bead just strung **(Figure 1)**. String 1 bead and pass through the next bead of the previous row and the bead just strung **(Figure 2)**. Repeat for the length of the row, stitching 1 new bead to each bead of the previous row **(Figure 3)**.

*Rows 3 and on:* Repeat Row 2 for a total of 16, 12, or 8 rows (according to the chart).

When you have finished each tile, remove the needle, secure the thread by weaving back through a few rows, and set the tile aside. Repeat Step 1 until all 5 tiles are completed.

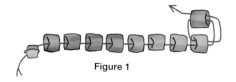

Figure 1

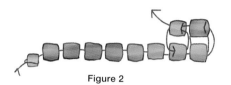

Figure 2

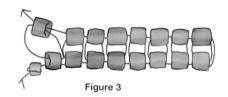

Figure 3

**Tip:**
If your square-stitched tile isn't quite square, you can even the tension by passing straight through each row, back and forth toward the first row; pass the tail thread through the first few rows, then secure each thread somewhere in the center of the tile, tying knots between beads, then trimming close.

**Small tile chart**

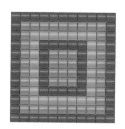

**Medium tile chart**

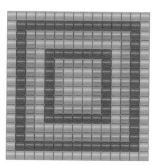

**Large tile chart**

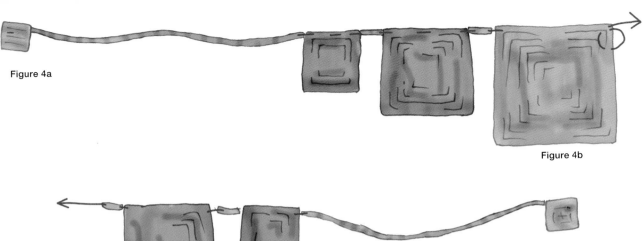

Figure 4a

Figure 4b

Figure 5

## Left side

**2.** Use 6' (2 m) of thread and size 8° beads to square-stitch a tile that is 4 beads wide and 4 rows long for the left half of the necklace **(Figure 4a)**. Pass back through each row to reinforce and snug the beads.

**3.** To connect the tiles, string 4" (10 cm) of size 11°s and pass through the top row of a 7-bead tile. String 1" (2.5 cm) of beads and pass through the top row of an 11-bead tile. String another 1" (2 cm) of beads and pass through the top row of the 15-bead tile. Snug the beads and pass through the edge bead in the previous row of the tile and through the last bead of the top row again to hold the beads in place **(Figure 4b)**; set aside.

## Right side

**4.** Repeat Step 2 to make a 4-bead tile for the right half of the necklace and connect the remaining 7- and 11-bead tiles **(Figure 5)**. Pass through the top row of the 15-bead tile in the opposite direction of the previous strand, then continue to pass back through the left strand to exit the first 4-bead tile. Pass the first thread back through the beads on the right to exit the second 4-bead tile.

*Getting Started with Seed Beads*

### Curving strands

**5.** For the second strand, use one of the threads to pass through the second row of the 4-bead tile, then string beads and pass through the second row of each tile to exit the opposite 4-bead tile. To create a curve, string each section 1 bead longer than the previous strand **(Figure 6)**. Pass the other thread back through the entire strand.

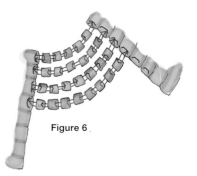

Figure 6

**6.** Work 2 more strands as before, adding 1 bead to each section and passing back through each strand with an opposite thread. Secure each thread by passing back through a strand, tying a few knots between beads, then trim.

### Clasp

**7.** Use 6' (2 m) of thread and size 11°s to work a peyote-stitched strip that is 12 beads wide and 12 rows long, following the directions for the Snappy Bands but stringing 12 beads instead of 8 (see page 72). Following the directions for Beaded Cylinder Beads, stitch the first and last rows together to form a tube (see page 77). Pass back through each row to reinforce and stiffen the beads; exit from the middle of a row.

Figure 7

**8.** String 5 size 11° beads and pass through the second row of one of the 4-bead tiles. Pass back through the third row, string 5 more size 11° beads, and pass through 2 beads of the tube to exit next to the first 5 beads. Pass through the beads again, working square stitches **(Figure 7)**; secure the thread and trim.

**9.** Secure a new thread in the other small end tile, exiting from the first row. String enough size 11° beads to form a loop that fits around one end of the toggle. Pass through the tile to exit the fourth row and string a second loop **(Figure 8)**. Weave through all the beads again to reinforce each loop, then secure the thread and trim.

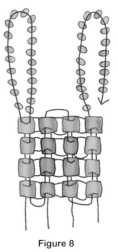

Figure 8

# Radiant Barrette

Square stitch doesn't have to be square. These circles are made of concentric rounds of square-stitched beads, with half circles worked off two sides of the final round. Accent the square-stitched circles with a hair stick trimmed in square-stitched corkscrew fringe. You'll never be square again!

## Materials

Size 8° seed beads (colors A, B, C, D)
Size 11° seed beads (colors E, F, G, H)
Needle and thread

Double-pointed needle (available in craft or knitting stores; choose U.S. sizes 6–8 [4–5mm])

## Barrette center circle

**1.** Work 9 rounds of circular square stitch with size 8° beads to make the center of the barrette.

*Round 1:* Use 6' (2 m) of thread to string 8A; pass through them again, leaving a 4" (10 cm) tail. Tie a knot with the tail and pass through the next bead.

*Round 2:* String 1A and 1B; pass through the bead the thread is exiting from and through the 2 beads just strung. String 1A and 1B; pass through the next bead of the previous round and through the beads just strung **(Figure 1)**. Repeat all around, stitching 2 beads to each bead of the previous round. Pass once through the entire round to snug the beads.

*Round 3:* String 1B and pass through the last bead of the previous round and through the bead just strung. String 1B and pass back through the next bead and through the bead just strung. String 2B and pass back through the next bead and through the bead just strung **(Figure 2)**. Repeat all around, working two stitches with 1 bead each followed by one stitch with 2 beads. Pass once through the entire round to snug the beads.

*Round 4:* Alternate 1B and 1C, work a 2-bead increase every fourth stitch—work three stitches with 1 bead, followed by one stitch with 2 beads.

*Round 5:* Using all C beads, work a 2-bead increase in every fifth stitch.

*Round 6:* Alternate 2C and 2B, increasing every sixth stitch.

*Round 7:* Use all B beads, increasing every seventh stitch.

*Round 8:* Alternate 1B and 1D, increasing every eighth stitch.

*Round 9:* Use all B beads, increasing every ninth stitch.

Figure 1

Figure 2

**TIP:** Depending on the width of the beads, you may need to work more or fewer 2-bead increases. To decide, check that the beads all radiate straight out from the center. When the beads in the round you are working start to tilt backward, work a 2-bead stitch; if the beads start to lean forward, tilting over the beads of the previous row, you are working too many 2-bead stitches.

Figure 3

Figure 4

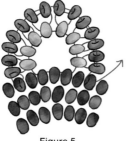

Figure 5

## Semicircles

**2.** Make a half circle, working arcs that attach at each end to the last round of the circle.

*Arc 1:* String 8D and pass through 3 beads of the last circle round and the beads just strung. Pass through 4 beads to exit next to the first bead just strung **(Figure 3)**.

*Arc 2:* Work 1B all around, increasing with a 2-bead stitch as necessary to keep the work flat **(Figure 4)**. When you reach the end of the arc, pass through the next bead of the last circle round, then back through all the beads of this arc and the next circle bead at the start **(Figure 5)**.

*Arcs 3–6:* Repeat Arc 2, using all C beads for Arc 3; all B for Arc 4; alternating 2A and 1B for Arc 5; and using all B for Arc 6.

Weave through the first and last arcs several times to reinforce, then secure the thread and trim.

Secure a new thread at the other side of the circle and repeat Step 2.

## Hair stick

**3.** With size 8°s, work a flat strip of square stitch that fits around the knitting needle, then embellish with corkscrew fringe made with size 11°s.

*Row 1:* String 1 bead and pass through it again to form a tension bead, leaving a 4" (10 cm) tail.  String 1B, 1C, 1B, 1D, 1B, 1C, and 1B.

*Rows 2–8:* Work square stitch, matching each bead color to the corresponding bead in the previous row. Work more or fewer rows as needed to reach around the knitting needle.

**4.** Wrap double-sided tape around the knitting needle about 2" (5 cm) from the end. Wrap the beaded band around it and stitch through beads in the first and last rows to connect the ends. Secure the thread and trim close.

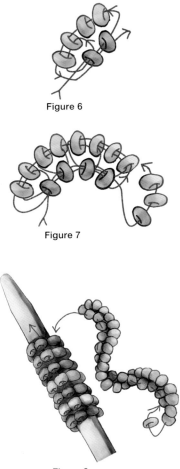

Figure 6

Figure 7

Figure 8

## Corkscrew fringe

**5.** Use 4' (1.2 m) of thread to string 1F and 2G and pass through them again, leaving a 6" (15 cm) tail; pass through the 1F again. *String 1F and 2G; pass through the last 2G, 1F, and the 1F just strung **(Figure 6)**. Repeat from * for the desired length, keeping the thread tension tight so that the G beads form a coil around the F beads **(Figure 7)**. When the coil is the desired length, string 1G and pass up through all the F beads **(Figure 8)**. Pass through a few beads on the hair stick band and the start of the corkscrew several times to secure, then weave through beads and trim close.

Repeat from Step 5 to make 2 more fringes, substituting E for B on one fringe and H for B on the other.

# Tubular Herringbone

Beads are stitched two at a time, neatly on top of a pair in the previous round to form columns that travel straight up, yet the thread travels through each round like a wave, making the stitch elusive and difficult to compare to other bead-weaving techniques.

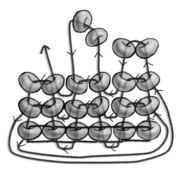

Placing beads two at a time gives herringbone stitch its distinctive tilt.

The projects in this chapter use ladder stitch as a base before beginning the first row of herringbone. You may want to brush up on your ladder stitch from page 85.

### Adding thread to herringbone

The flexible nature of this stitch requires some care when ending or starting thread: A secured thread could easily wiggle loose, while an overly secured thread would stiffen the beads and take away the luxurious drape. To make it tight, while staying loose, stop when your working thread is less than 6" (15 cm); finish working the round and step up through 2 beads for the next round. Instead of stringing beads, tie a half hitch knot around the thread at the top of the first column. Pull tight and pass down through several beads of the same column, leaving a tail thread. Prepare a new thread and pass up through several beads to exit from the first bead of the round and tie a knot at the same place. Follow the thread path of the last round: pass down through 2 beads, then up through 2 beads to exit the top of the second column. Tie a half hitch knot, and continue around (pass down through 2, up through 2, tie a knot at the top of the third column). Step up and resume beading. Trim the tail of the old thread or weave through and knot between a few beads.

# Squishy Rings

## Materials

Size 11° seed beads (A and B)
Beading needle and thread

Herringbone stitch works up into a beaded tube so smooth it will have you wrapped around its finger. Better yet, wrap the tube around your own finger and wear it as a ring. Changing the way you work with color could change the way you look at this stitch—sample the two methods below to make a different ring for each hand.

Figure 1

Figure 2

Figure 3

Figure 4

## Horizontally striped rings

**1.** To make a ladder-stitched foundation round, use 6' (2 m) of thread and string 2A and 2B, then pass through the beads again, leaving a 6" (15 cm) tail. *String 2A and pass through the last 2B and the 2A just strung. String 2B and pass through the last 2A and the 2B just strung. Repeat once from * so that you have six 2-bead stacks **(Figure 1)**. Pass through the first 2A, the last 2B, and the first 2A again to make a ring, with the tail thread at the bottom **(Figure 2)**.

*Round 1:* String 1A and 1B; pass down through the next 1B and up through the following 1A of the previous round **(Figure 3)**. Repeat twice. After passing down through the last 1B of the previous round, step up for the next round by passing up through 2A to exit from the first bead of this round **(Figure 4)**.

### Stepping up

To work a herringbone tube with straight columns, you must step up at the end of each round. Because the beads are tilted, you may not easily notice when you are finished with a round, even when working only a few beads. Make use of color changes to make the step up obvious.

*Getting Started with Seed Beads*

**2.** Continue as in Round 1, matching the new beads to the beads below them to create solid color columns (**Figure 5**). Step up by passing up through 2 beads. After a few rounds, the tops of the columns will spread apart like a banana, coming back together as each round is worked.

**3.** Work a tube long enough to wrap around your finger. To make a ring, join the ends by aligning the columns (A to A and B to B), then pass up through 1A in the first round, then down through the following 1B and the next 1B in the last round (**Figure 6**). Continue around, passing up through 2A and down 2B to connect the first and last rounds. Weave through beads to secure the thread and trim.

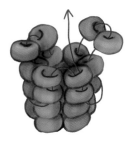

Figure 5

Figure 6

### Vertically striped rings

**1.** Use 6' (2 m) of thread to make a ladder of six 2-bead stacks using all A beads. Stitch the first and last stacks together to form a ring (**Figure 1**).

*Round 1:* String 2B; pass down through the next 1A, up through the following 1A, and pull snug. Repeat twice and step up by passing through 1A of the previous round and the first 1B of this round (**Figure 2**).

Figure 1

Figure 2

Figure 3

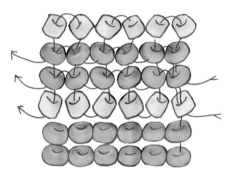

Figure 4

*Round 2:* String 2A; pass down through the next 1B of the previous round, up through the following 1B, and pull snug. Repeat twice and step up by passing through 1B of the previous round and the first 1A of this round **(Figure 3)**.

*Round 3:* String 2A; pass down through the next 1A of the previous round, up through the following 1A, and pull snug. Repeat twice and step up by passing through 1A of the previous round and the first 1A of this round.

**2.** Repeat from Round 1, working one round with 2B in each stitch, followed by two rounds with 2A in each stitch, for the desired length **(Figure 4)**.

**3.** Work a tube long enough to wrap around your finger, then connect the ends as described for the horizontally striped ring, taking care that the columns are lined up (even though they are not the same color for their whole length).

*Getting Started with Seed Beads*

# Tripod Earrings

## Materials

Size 11° hex beads (A)

Size 11° round beads (B)

Size 15° round beads (C)

Pair of ear wires

Needle and thread

Spread columns of herring-bone stitch apart by stringing beads between them. Increase the number of beads added with each round, and the tube will flare out like an umbrella. These tubular-stitched earrings use hex and round seed beads to emphasize the interesting structure.

1. *Ladder base:* Use 6' (2 m) of thread to string 4A and pass through them again, leaving a 4" (10 cm) tail. String 2A and pass through the last 2A and the 2A just strung; repeat four times to make a ladder that is 2 beads high and 6 beads wide (**Figure 1**). Pass through the first and last pairs of beads to join the ends together (**Figure 2**).

Figure 1

Figure 2

Figure 3

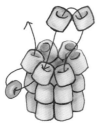

Figure 4

Figure 5

Figure 6

**Round 1:** String 2A and pass down through the next 1A and up through the following 1A. Repeat twice and step up for the next round by passing through the first 1A of this round **(Figure 3)**.

**Round 2:** String 2A and pass down through the next 1A of the previous round. String 1B and pass up through the next 1A **(Figure 4)**. Repeat twice and step up for the next round by passing up through 2A **(Figure 5)**.

**Round 3:** String 2A and pass down through the next 1A of the previous round. String 2B and pass up through the next 1A. Repeat twice and step up for the next round by passing up through 2A **(Figure 6)**.

**Rounds 4–8:** Increase each round by adding 1B to each stitch for a total of 7B in the seventh round.

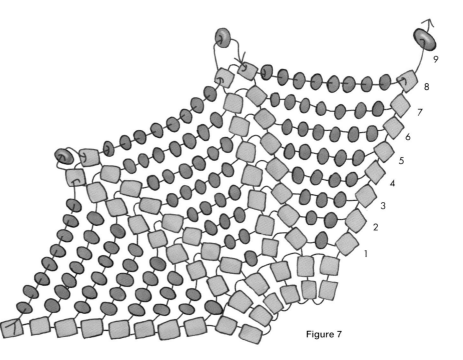

Figure 7

***Round 9:*** String 1B and pass down through the next 1A of the previous round, forming a tip at the end of the column. String 8B and pass up through the next 1A. Repeat twice, stringing 1B, then 8B, for each stitch **(Figure 7)**. Pass through all of the beads in this round again to reinforce.

**2.** Work beads to close up the start of the tube. Turn the work around (which will be right side up, with the small end at the top, in the finished piece) and pass up through all the beads in the second bead of one column to exit from the other side of the ladder-stitched base round. String 1B and pass down through the next column of beads, through the 1B at the tip, and up through the other half of column **(Figure 8a)**. Repeat twice to stitch 1B between every other bead around the top of the ladder.

**3.** Pass through the 3B just added, then pass through them again to snug them together. String 8C and one ear wire. Skip 1B, pass through the next 1B, and pull snug to form a loop **(Figure 8b)**. Pass through the loop of beads again to reinforce, then weave through beads to secure the thread and trim.

Repeat from Step 1 to make the second earring.

Figure 8

# Wickedly Smooth Lariat

Even if you don't make a habit of wearing lariats as jewelry, you might want to make one as an excuse to take advantage of this luxurious stitch. This one uses both round- and hex-shaped seed beads to show off the intricate herringbone pattern.

**Materials**
Size 11° metallic round and
metallic matte hex beads
in 3 colors each
Beading needle and thread

1. Follow the instructions for a vertically striped ring (Steps 1–2, page 116) to make a 6-bead tube for 39" (99 cm).

2. Finish the end of the tube with 8 increasing rounds, working flares between stitches as for the tripod earrings (Rounds 2–9, pages 120–121). Secure a thread at the start of the tube and work eight rounds off the other end. Weave through the flared rounds to reinforce, secure the thread, and trim close.

# Twisted Cable Bracelet

## Materials

Size 8° seed beads in 2 to 4 colors

1" (2 cm) button

Needle and thread

### Herringbone spiral tube

**1.** *Ladder base:* Work a 2-bead ladder that is 6 columns long, changing colors for each column **(Figure 1)**. Pass through the first and last columns to join the ends.

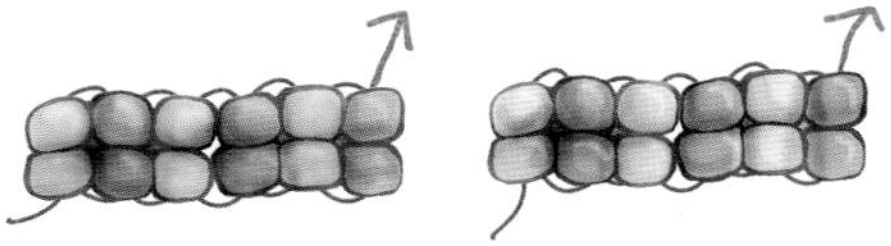

**Figure 1**

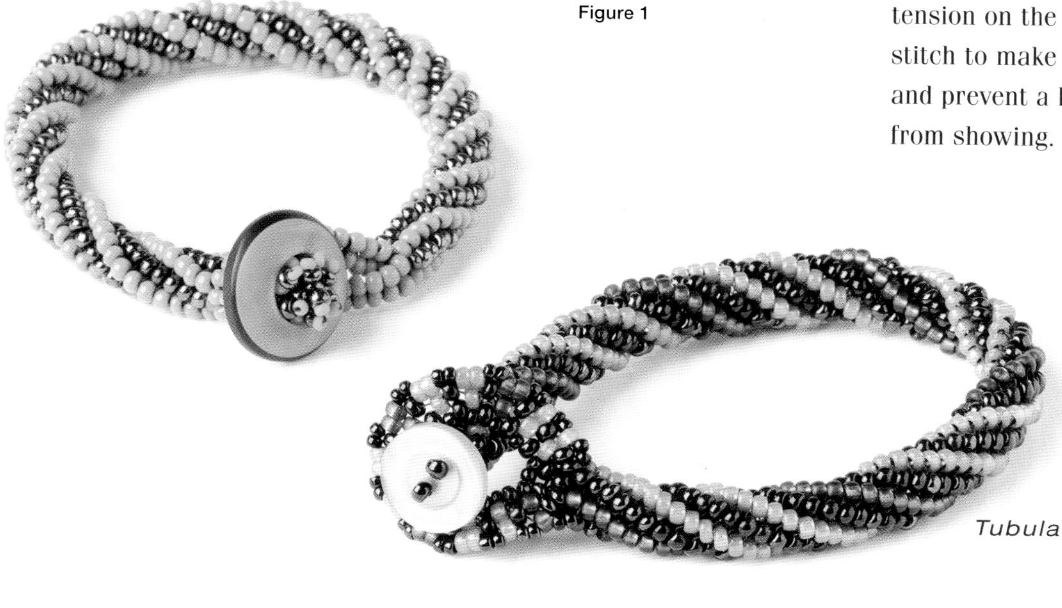

Working a herringbone tube with consistently uneven stitches (down one and up three) causes the columns to bend, forming a spiral that looks like a twined rope. You don't need to worry about stepping up each round when working a spiral, so choose your stripe sequence for the foundation round and just follow it around and around. You will need to keep fairly tight tension on the thread in this stitch to make the tube spiral and prevent a lot of thread from showing.

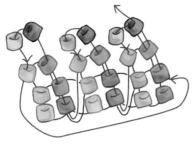

Figure 2

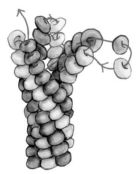

Figure 3

Figure 4

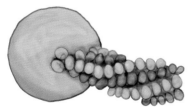

Figure 5

**Round 1:** String 2 beads (first bead the color of the column that the thread is exiting from, second bead the color of the next column) and pass down through the next bead and up through the following 2 beads; repeat twice, passing up through 3 beads at the end of the round **(Figure 2)**.

**Rounds 2 and on:** String 2 beads and pass down through 1 bead and up through 3 beads; repeat twice, passing up through 3 beads at the end of the round **(Figure 3)**. Don't worry about stepping up each round; just pass up through 3 beads for each stitch until the rope is the desired length.

**Next round:** Work one round stringing 2 beads, passing down through 1 bead, and up through 2 beads for each stitch.

**Decrease round:** String 1 bead and pass down through 1 bead and up through 1 bead for each stitch (3 beads total). Pass through the 3 single beads and pull snug to cinch the end of the tube. Set the thread aside to work the clasp loop in Step 3.

**2. Button:** Use the tail thread to work a decrease round (3 beads total). String 2 beads and the button; pass through the opposite hole of the button, string 2 beads, and pass through beads at the end of the tube **(Figure 4)**. Weave through the beads and button several times to reinforce, secure the thread, and trim.

**3. Loop:** Exiting from the last decrease round at the other end of the bracelet, string 2 beads and pass back through the next bead in the last round and the bead the thread is exiting from; pull snug. *String 2 beads and pass through the second, then the first beads just worked; pull snug and pass through the first bead just strung. Repeat from * to work a 2-bead strap long enough to fit over the clasp button. Secure the end by passing through beads on the opposite side of the tube, then pass through the loop and tube a few times to reinforce **(Figure 5)**. Secure the thread and trim.

*Getting Started with Seed Beads*

# Peyote loop variation

Instead of working the loop as in Step 3, form a loop of beads (size 8°
and 11°), then work rounds of peyote stitch for a colorful ending:

***Round 1:*** String 1 size 8° and 1 size 11° ten times (or enough to fit
around the button). String 1 size 8° and pass through the end of the
tube to exit from the first bead of the loop **(Figure 1)**.

***Round 2:*** String 1 size 8° and pass through the next size 8° of the previous round; repeat around, then weave through the end of the tube to
exit the first bead of this round **(Figure 2)**.

***Round 3:*** Repeat Round 2 **(Figure 3)**.

***Round 4:*** String 2 size 11°s and pass through the next size 8°; repeat
around **(Figure 4)**. Pass through the round again to reinforce, then
secure the thread and trim.

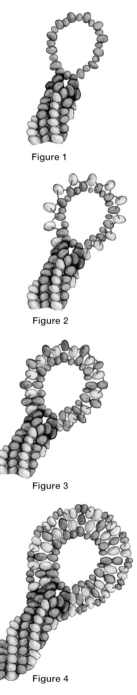

Figure 1

Figure 2

Figure 3

Figure 4

# Resources

## BEAD SOURCES

Your local bead store is a source of materials and information, with staff that are usually well versed in beadworking techniques and tips. Mine is:

**Bead Cache**
3307 S. College Ave.
Fort Collins, CO 80525
(970) 224-4322

Other resources for this book are available from the following stores:

**Orr's Trading**
3422 S. Broadway
Englewood, CO 80110
(303) 722-6466; www.orrs.com

**Beyond Beadery**
PO Box 460
Rollinsville, CO 80474
Toll-free: (800) 840-5548,
Fax: (866) FAX-BEAD
www.beyondbeadery.com

**Jane's Fiber & Beads**
5415 E. Andrew Johnson Hwy.
PO Box 110
Afton, TN 37616
Toll-free: (888) 497-2665;
Fax: (423) 638-5676
www.janesfibersandbeads.com

**Cartwright's Sequins**
www.ccartwright.com

**Specialty Bottle**
(206) 340-0459
www.specialtybottle.com
(clean, blank tins for Bead Soup Cans)

# FURTHER READING

Campbell, Jean, and Judith Durant. *The New Beader's Companion.* Loveland, Colorado: Interweave Press, 2005.

Cypher, Carol Huber. *Mastering Beadwork: A Comprehensive Guide to Off-Loom Techniques.* Loveland, Colorado: Interweave Press, 2007.

Dean, David. *Beading in the Native American Tradition.* Loveland, Colorado: Interweave Press, 2002.

Deeb, Margie. *The Beader's Guide to Color.* New York: Watson-Guptill Publications, 2004.

Hector, Valerie, and Lois Sherr Dubin. *The Art of Beadwork: Historic Inspiration, Contemporary Design.* New York: Watson-Guptill Publications, 2005.

*500 Beaded Objects: New Dimensions in Contemporary Beadwork.* Asheville, North Carolina: Lark Books, 2004.

McKinnon, Kate. *Project Workbook 2003.* Available from the author at katemckinnon.com or by writing to her at PO Box 153, Pacific Grove, CA 93950.

Menz, Deb. *Colorworks: The Crafter's Guide to Color.* Loveland, Colorado: Interweave Press, 2004.

*Beadwork* How-To Series. Loveland, Colorado: Interweave Press.

> Clarke, Amy C., and Robin Atkins. *Beaded Embellishment.*
>
> Cook, Jeanette, and Vicki Star. *Beading with Peyote Stitch.*
>
> Fitzgerald, Diane. *Beading with Brick Stitch.*
>
> Fitzgerald, Diane. *Netted Beadwork.*
>
> Star, Vicki. *Beading with Herringbone Stitch.*

Seek out a local guild or bead society; you don't have to be an expert to belong to one of these communities. Don't forget to volunteer your time; you'll be greatly appreciated.

# INDEX